IMPACT STATEMENT

A Family's Fight for Justice against
Whitey Bulger, Stephen Flemmi, and the FBI

Bob Halloran

SKYHORSE PUBLISHING

This book is dedicated to the memory of my sister,
Debbie Davis—always loved, never forgotten.

—Steve Davis

Skyhorse Publishing books may be purchased in bulk at special discounts for sales promotion, corporate gifts, fund-raising, or educational purposes. Special editions can also be created to specifications. For details, contact the Special Sales Department, Skyhorse Publishing, 307 West 36th Street, 11th Floor, New York, NY 10018 or info@skyhorsepublishing.com.

Skyhorse® and Skyhorse Publishing® are registered trademarks of Skyhorse Publishing, Inc.®, a Delaware corporation.

Visit our website at www.skyhorsepublishing.com.

10 9 8 7 6 5 4 3 2 1

Library of Congress Cataloging-in-Publication Data is available on file.

ISBN: 978-1-62636-033-4

Printed in the United States

CONTENTS

CONTENTS

INTRODUCTION

In this book you're going to meet a man named Steve Davis. Hopefully your experience is better than the one I had the first time I met him. With his gravelly voice, he invited me to sit down at his kitchen table, and even with his gracious manner and his offer of an assorted cheese platter, I felt a little intimidated. Steve is a sweetheart of a guy, but he likes to hide that fact for as long as possible. Perhaps it's because he doesn't trust people and has trouble calling anyone his friend. But those walls eventually came down between us, and now he's my friend—the kind who likes to drop by unannounced, either to bring me something (like a large fresh tuna "a guy he knows" caught), or to use the bathroom on his way to somewhere else.

That first introduction I had with Steve was his attempt to size me up as the potential author of this book. I have no idea what he was looking for. Compatibility, most likely. He certainly didn't ask for any writing samples, or check out my resume, but by the time the cheese platter had settled into the pits of our stomachs, we were partners.

I told Steve my goal was to write a vastly different kind of "Whitey Bulger" book, one that connected readers emotionally to a single, sympathetic character. Instead of focusing on a multitude of crimes that were both horrific and fascinating, I would tell the story of an innocent, young woman whose life was tragically taken away. Steve's sister Debbie would be my protagonist. Her story would be the fulcrum to the rest of the Whitey Bulger story. But as I was writing, a funny thing happened along the way; another sympathetic character began to materialize. And it was Steve Davis.

As I learned more about his story, the book began to develop a dual focus. Steve and Debbie were very close as children. They protected each other from an extremely abusive father. They both left their home as teenagers—Steve when he was thrown out at age fifteen and Debbie when she married at age sixteen. Steve sold drugs to survive. Debbie divorced and became Steve Flemmi's prized trophy. And when Debbie mysteriously disappeared, Steve Davis embarked upon the fight of his life, and it's likely to be a fight for the rest of his life. Personally, I hope he gives it up so that his anger will finally subside, and he can concentrate on all the love he has for his friends and his family.

In the early stages of writing, I referred to him as "Every Day Steve" because he called every day with a different idea or story for the book. Sometimes I happily wrote them down; usually though, I just pretended to. But the nickname "Every Day Steve" eventually became a compliment with the highest respect. That guy was in the courtroom every day, all day, all summer long! He didn't do it for the attention, or for money. He did it because the best fighters never skip a day of training. Their dedication is evident every day.

A good portion of this book was written before Whitey Bulger's trial began in June 2013. Structurally, it breaks down into three parts. First, there's the backstory of the Davis family, and they're a wild bunch, to say the least. Then there's the discovery of Debbie's body, which intensified the family's fight for justice through the courts. And finally, there's Bulger's trial, which Steve and I attended every day and discussed every night.

It was an untitled manuscript until the day Steve and I drove to the courthouse together for the sentencing of Bulger's girlfriend, Catherine Greig, in May 2013. Steve was scheduled to deliver a victim impact statement, which is when a victim's family member is allowed to address the court to explain how his or her life has been impacted by the guilty party's crime. By then I knew the Davises suspected Flemmi and Bulger for the deaths of their father, Eddie, a brother named Ronnie, and two sisters, Debbie and Michelle. The light bulb switched on, and *Impact Statement* was born.

CHAPTER ONE

Meeting at Triple O's

Steve Davis heard the question clearly. It was spoken softly, but firmly and uncomfortably close to his ear. In his mind he could hear the question repeated again and again, growing in volume each time. But he didn't respond. He was fixated on the .357 Magnum on the desk in front of him, and the body bag on the floor.

Why had he left his gun in the car?

His eyes darted from the gun to the body bag as he felt the warmth of a hand on the back of his neck, the fingers squeezing with surprising force. His eyes were still adjusting to the darkness of the room, and the question lingered, suspended in the air. Steve considered a series of responses, but the courage required to utter a single syllable momentarily escaped him. The drug dealing, street-tough wiseass was smart enough to know this was the time for a measured reply, or none at all. Before he spoke, the question came firing at him even more forcefully.

"What's your life worth?"

The first time Whitey Bulger asked him the question there was a convivial tone that conveyed genuine curiosity, as if he really wanted to know what value the twenty-something-year-old kid placed on his life. But Whitey Bulger didn't like to repeat himself, and the second time he asked, he bellowed, and there was more than a hint of intimidation. He thought the gun and the body bag would have been enough, but if this punk didn't even show him enough respect to answer a god-damn question then things would have to get rough. Bulger's reputation as a stone-cold killer was well earned, and it was well-known by Steve Davis, who had the misfortune of being called on this day to answer to Whitey.

Davis had never pondered what his life was worth, and he still wasn't giving it much thought now. Instead, his mind kept repeating: "Why the fuck did I leave my gun in the car?"

Just a few minutes earlier, Bulger had been peering out the window of Triple O's, a popular neighborhood bar in South Boston. He pulled back a curtain and saw a relatively new 1979 red Camaro pull up with Davis in the passenger seat. Bulger liked his prey to be on time, and he smiled just a little.

Satisfied, Bulger calmly turned and made his way to the office on the second floor. It was eleven o'clock in the morning, and Triple O's was nearly empty. Bulger, Steve Flemmi, Kevin Weeks, and a short, ugly bartender were the only people in the bar. In a few hours, the place would be filled with men and women from the neighborhood, regulars who sat on the stools, drinking their paychecks away night after night, wondering if the word on the street was accurate and that Bulger really did have bodies buried right below them in the basement.

"Send him up," was all Bulger said.

Weeks, the bar's bouncer and Bulger's muscle, nodded to Flemmi. Neither man spoke, but each of them wondered how this one was going to play out. They knew that would be entirely up to Steve Davis, the prey who remained in the sports car outside.

The Camaro was one of three cars Davis owned. It was three years old, but cherry. The other two cars were Cadillacs. He also had a motorcycle, gold jewelry, and a big drawer full of money, though there was less of it ever since he started dating Susan Culhane. She didn't have particularly expensive taste, but Davis couldn't resist showing off. He even had Susan's name written in gold letters on the quarter panel of the Camaro. If he happened to break up with Susan, he could always get a new car. The cocaine business was that good.

The first time Davis had ever heard of cocaine, he had to ask what a person does with it. It wasn't long after that he was buying it for $20,000 a week and selling it for up to $65,000. Basically, he knew a guy who knew a guy with a direct connection to people in Columbia. Knowing that Bulger controlled South Boston, Davis sold exclusively in nearby Hyde Park. Unbeknownst to Davis, his own brother, Mickey, whom he'd brought in as a favor to their mom, had started selling in Bulger's jurisdiction. So, when Flemmi summoned Davis for an audience with Bulger, he didn't know why Bulger wanted to see him, but he figured it couldn't be good. His suspicious mind, the one that crossed over the border into paranoia, began racing erratically the moment Flemmi proffered the invitation. Davis was at a Dunkin' Donuts off Morrissey Boulevard in Dorchester when Flemmi approached.

"Jimmy wants to see you," Flemmi told him.

"Jimmy? Who the fuck is Jimmy?"

"It's Whitey. We don't call him Whitey."

"Well, that's the only way I know him," Davis said. "What's Whitey want with me?"

"Just wants to see you. What do you say we go for a ride?"

Davis's antennae shot straight up, and he was immediately dialed into the danger. For it was Flemmi himself, some years earlier who had advised him, "Any time a guy you're not sure is your friend says, 'Let's go for a ride,' don't go. That phrase is used to indicate it's your last ride."

Davis took that advice to heart, and as Flemmi sat across the table from him, he couldn't be sure if Flemmi was his friend. Too much had happened in the last year.

"I'm gonna have to pass," Davis responded. "You see, a guy once told me not to get in a car with someone I wasn't sure about."

Flemmi actually got a kick out of hearing his own words come back to him. He smiled and gave a slight nod of approval. He nodded again when Davis told him he could make it over to see Bulger the next day. Davis showed up knowing that when he went in he had about a fifty-fifty chance of coming out.

"He'll kill you if he sees that," Mark Caravan said as Davis pulled a gun out from under his seat. Mark was a good friend who agreed to drive Davis to his showdown with Bulger.

"The only time he's gonna see it is right before I kill him," Davis said. "I ain't going in there without being able to protect myself."

Davis stuffed the gun into the waistband of his sweatpants, but Mark persisted. He thought Steve was crazy to go into a meeting with Whitey Bulger packing, and he told him so. Their argument lasted several minutes.

"Listen," Davis said to Mark, "if I'm not back in thirty minutes, get the fuck out of here, and call someone. Call the police. Call my mother. I don't give a fuck. But tell 'em to get here in a hurry before these guys dump my body somewheres."

Davis checked the gun for bullets, spun the cylinder, and looked toward the front door of Triple O's. He saw Flemmi looking back at him. He'd known Flemmi for a while, first hearing his father speak at the dinner table about the nefarious Winter Hill Gang, and later seeing Flemmi's picture on a wanted poster at the police station. As a young adult, Davis got to know Flemmi on a personal basis, and came to admire him. He watched him closely and learned from him. Father figure? Possibly. But he was definitely a role model for Davis in the way that bad guys emulate other bad guys.

Flemmi had also dated Steve's sister, Debbie, for the better part of seven years. Flemmi was much older than Debbie. He was also married, and a known killer, but Steve liked him anyway. He never trusted him, and even less so now, but he had always liked him enough to talk to.

Seeing Flemmi look back at him offered no comfort. If something bad were going to happen, Flemmi wouldn't have the back of his ex-mistress's brother. Flemmi's loyalty was to Bulger, his longtime partner in crime.

Now, as Davis opened the door and swung his leg out of the car, he paused and reached once again for his gun. Keeping it hidden behind the door, Davis abruptly shoved the gun back under his seat and slammed the door. Not knowing why he ultimately relented to Mark's wisdom, he marched determinedly to the entrance of Triple O's.

Mark watched him go. He was undoubtedly more concerned about his friend's well-being than the unsuspecting Brian Halloran was when he parked in nearly the exact same spot two years earlier. On that day, Halloran watched Louis Litif walk toward the same door—and unwittingly toward his own death. Litif, a South Boston bookmaker, had similarly been summoned by Bulger to Triple O's. Halloran gave Litif a ride, watched him go in, and then watched him come out wrapped inside a green trash bag. Litif's body would be found days later stuffed in the trunk of his new Lincoln. He'd been stabbed several times with an ice pick, and shot in the head, probably in that order.

"Maybe," Mark thought, "Steve should have brought the gun with him after all."

Whatever fear Davis felt was being smothered by attitude and bravado. Regularly beaten by his father since he was five, and out on his own since he was fourteen, Davis didn't take shit from anyone. Then again, Bulger wasn't just anyone.

"Where the hell is he?" Bulger must have wondered.

Bulger had positioned himself behind a small desk in an office at the far end of the second floor. The lights were off and the only available light was provided by that morning's overcast skies, just a few streaks of sunlight coming through a small window partially blocked by dark curtains. Bulger was used to the darkness, having spent three years in a tiny cell at Alcatraz for robbing a bank, and having spent most of his adult life lurking in shadows. The darkness would be an advantage for him now. He was intricately aware of the confines and dimensions of this office. Triple O's was owned by Kevin O'Neil, but Bulger treated it as his own. O'Neil was once represented by Whitey's brother, Billy Bulger, on a murder charge and Billy got the charges dismissed. So, there was not only a friendship, but also a debt. Whitey had executed dozens of business deals from inside Triple O's, and he was ready to conduct another, or he was ready for the alternative.

Whitey sat with his back to the wall. He unzipped the body bag to his left, and placed his .357 Magnum and two bullets on the desk. He liked the clear message of a perfectly prepared staging, and no mob cliché was off limits. Whitey was nothing if not a drama queen. Certain that everything was just right, Whitey closed his eyes and waited. And he waited. Several minutes went by, and Whitey was losing his patience.

"Where is he?" Davis asked as he sauntered into Triple O's.

"Jimmy's upstairs," Flemmi responded. "He's waiting for ya."

"What's this all about?"

"You'll find out soon enough."

Davis walked toward the back of the bar where Weeks was standing at the foot of the stairs.

"Up there?" Steve asked. "It's fuckin' pitch black. What are you guys up to?"

Davis didn't get a response. He also wasn't patted down, so right away he knew he could have brought his gun in with him. He wished he had it now. Davis walked carefully up the stairs. His caution was a product of not knowing if he was about to take a bullet when he reached the top of the stairs, and because he truly couldn't see where he was going. With his foot firmly on the top stair, Davis turned, waited for his eyes to focus, and recognized Whitey sitting behind the desk. Whitey didn't speak. He merely motioned for Steve to sit in the chair adjacent to the desk. As Davis approached, he saw the gun, the bullets, and the body bag just as Whitey had placed them.

Then there was the question: "What is your life worth?" Davis was still hearing it reverberate in his head. He was certain it was a question Whitey had asked dozens, maybe hundreds of others he had shaken down in the past. Had any of them given the right answer?

"I guess it's worth whatever you tell me it is," Steve said, his right leg involuntarily tapping like an excited dog's.

For his part, Bulger continuously flipped one of the bullets between his fingers and stood it up straight on the desk. He'd tap it a few times and begin the process all over again. There was a methodical rhythm to it. Suddenly, Whitey picked up the .357, jumped out from behind the desk, and grabbed Steve behind the neck. He popped Steve in the mouth with the gun causing two little pieces of tooth to fall out and onto the desk. "I'll tell you what it's worth," Bulger barked. "Five thousand a week."

"I ain't got that."

"Fuck, you don't. Five thousand. Every week."

"I ain't got it. And even if I did, what would I get for it?"

"You get to live, asshole!"

Davis, of course, had the money, but he was determined not to give it to Whitey. He'd die first. And that was becoming a distinct possibility.

"You been dealing in South Boston," Whitey accused.

"No, I ain't. I'm Hyde Park. I ain't stupid."

"I'm telling you, you're in South Boston. And that's gonna cost you five grand a week."

Whitey's grip hadn't lessened at all. If anything, it tightened as he spoke. Bulger was slender, but strong; smallish, but powerful. Davis was even shorter, but thicker; barrel-chested. His adrenaline rush was all fear, while Bulger's was rage resulting in power. Davis felt the fingers on his neck, the cold gun on his cheek, and the pain in his tooth. But what he really felt was his fear yielding to his own level of rage. It was becoming increasingly clear that this was Mickey's fault. His screw-up of a brother must have screwed up again. He was infuriated with Mickey, and his blood boiled because he knew he couldn't explain it to Whitey. "You never rat on anybody," Davis's father had repeated many times. And Davis lived by that credo. It was perhaps the only time he'd ever listened to his father, the physically abusive drunk whom he had learned to hate by the time he was five years old. "I ain't got that kind of money," Davis lied again.

Whitey sized him up for a good, long time. He knew Davis had the money, but he was starting to believe Davis had no idea his drugs had crossed over to South Boston. "Tell you what," Whitey said at last. "You send your brother, Mickey, in to see me, and we'll table this little matter for the time being." Whitey pulled the gun away and released his grip on Davis's neck. But before Davis got up to leave, Whitey had one more surprise. He picked up one of the bullets and held it sideways in front of Davis's face. "This one's for you," Whitey said handing him the bullet. "It's got your name on it. And this other one here is for your brother." The cold-blooded killer certainly had a penchant for theatrics.

Incensed, but thankful to be getting out alive, Davis took the bullet, bolted upright, and headed back into the darkness of the staircase. Was he about to take the bullet with his name on it in the back of the head? Were Weeks and Flemmi waiting to kill him downstairs? These were the questions that filled him with so much adrenaline that when he got downstairs and discovered he wasn't going to be executed, he got right up in Flemmi's face. "You motherfucker! You knew what that was all about, and you sent me up into that fucking lion's den anyway! Fuck you! We're supposed to be friends!"

Flemmi let that last word settle before he spoke. Friends? Flemmi wasn't sure what it even meant any more. He had friends when he was a kid, but he had spent his entire adult life acquiring associates and business partners. He didn't trust any of them, and he was well aware they didn't trust him. There were no friends in the organized crime business. There were merely people who needed you, owed you a favor, or acted like friends until that didn't suit them anymore.

Again, Flemmi was standing in the very bar where his former "associate" Louis Litif, had been killed. Litif worked with and for Bulger for many years, but the relationship went awry when Litif started using profits from his gambling operation to buy and sell cocaine, but he didn't cut Bulger in on the action. Additionally, Litif committed a couple of murders that Bulger didn't approve of. The first was Litif's own business partner, Jimmy Matera.

The two of them owned Hap's Lounge in South Boston, and during an after-hours card game there one night, Matera thought he caught Litif cheating, so he slapped him across the face. A week later, Litif brought Matera down to the basement of Hap's to check on the water meter. While Matera read the meter, Litif shot him in the back of the head. The bartender upstairs, Robert Conrad, heard the shot, which meant he knew too much. Litif, as an act of friendship, brought Conrad on a vacation to Las Vegas and Nova Scotia where he got him drunk, killed him with a knife, and buried his body. The friendship was officially over.

Litif was ultimately killed on April 12, 1980. He called his wife, Ana, around noon and asked to borrow her car. His stomach was upset and he wanted to go out and buy some Maalox. The next day, the police went to the Litif's house and asked Ana if her car had been stolen, because they had found it abandoned in the South End of Boston. Ana didn't mention that Louie hadn't come home the night before, because he often stayed out all night. In addition to being married to Ana, Louie was living with another woman. When Ana found her car, she opened the trunk and found Louie wrapped inside a dark, green garbage bag. His Nike track suit was completely covered in his own blood. He had been stabbed thirty-eight times in the chest and stomach. Decades later, Flemmi swore under oath he didn't know who killed Louie Litif, but acknowledged "Bulger was happy that he was murdered. He didn't like him." A week prior to his murder, Litif had gotten into an argument with Bulger during which Bulger announced they were no longer friends.

So, it was strange for Steve Davis to use the word "friend," but it made Flemmi smile—not because he was happy to have a friend, but because it meant Davis was the fool he always thought him to be. Davis not only didn't know, he didn't even suspect.

"Get the hell out," Flemmi said flatly.

Weeks sidled up closer to Davis, an obvious effort to intimidate, just in case Davis had some crazy idea about taking a swing at Flemmi. Weeks never touched Davis. He just stood close by with his arms folded across his burly chest, and let his presence be known. Davis, who was also more chest than legs, was aware of Weeks, but indifferent to him. He had just survived a meeting with Whitey Bulger. Neither of these two gimokes was going to do anything without Whitey's permission. Davis felt safer now. But he was pissed.

When Davis got to his car, Mark Caravan was tapping his fingers on the steering wheel to the beat of a song on the radio. Equally nervous and curious, Mark waited for Davis to get in the car before turning the key further to start the engine. "How'd it go?" would have been the obvious question, but Mark didn't ask. Instead, he watched as Davis inhaled deliberately and exhaled loudly several times. Finally, Davis opened his beefy hand and revealed the large gold colored bullet. Mark recognized it as a .357 Magnum. "What's that?" he asked instead.

"Motherfucker gave me a bullet. Said this one's got my name on it and he's got another one with my brother Mickey's name on it. Fuck him. I got bullets, too. And a whole bunch of 'em have his name on 'em!" Davis tossed the bullet into the open ashtray of the car, and Mark peeled out of the parking lot.

Davis explained what happened. He told Mark about the gun, the threat, and the body bag. He bragged about his bravery and embellished within reason. Mark was appropriately impressed.

"That is one evil bastard!" Mark declared. He was talking about Bulger, but Davis was thinking about Flemmi, and he nodded. Davis knew what he was doing when he called Flemmi a friend. He had to make Flemmi feel safe. He couldn't let Flemmi know all the things he suspected. He couldn't prove anything yet, but he knew in his aching heart the enduring impact Flemmi and Bulger had on his family.

Davis looked out the car window and let the familiar parks, street corners, schools, and houses flood his mind with memories. Some of them were even good memories. Right over there was where Tommy Latorneau won the most vicious fight Steve had ever witnessed. Tommy earned the right to go out with Davis's sister, Debbie, and would eventually marry her. Watching two boys beat each other for almost an hour, delivering and withstanding punishment, gaining respect for one another as their faces swelled—that was a great memory. As Mark drove, Steve reminisced. Passing Jamaica Pond, Steve recalled the near fatal car accident his brother, Mickey, caused.

The woman was really hurt, Steve thought. *She didn't die, but her face and ribs were bad*. Mickey was driving, but didn't have his license with him. He ordered Steve to run home and get his license, but then didn't hang around the accident scene. When Steve returned, he was picked up by the police and taken in for questioning.

"Were you in the car?" a detective bellowed.

"No."

"What are you doing with this license?"

"I found it."

"Where's your brother?"

"I want to see my attorney."

Steve was thirteen years old. He knew to ask for an attorney, because he'd been instructed at an early age that he should lawyer up if he ever found himself in trouble. Not exactly typical advice for every adolescent. His mother picked him up and brought him home where he found his father enraged thinking that he had ratted out Mickey. Steve tried to explain that he hadn't told the cops anything, but since there was a warrant out for Mickey, his father assumed the worst. He beat Steve unceasingly until Mickey strolled through the door and confirmed Steve's story. The nearly exhausted father may have actually felt badly about what he'd just done, so he hugged his bloody son. That was not a good memory.

The drive continued. Over there was where he and his older brother, Ronnie, pulled off one of their first robberies. *Ronnie*, he thought wistfully. *First Ronnie, then Debbie.* His anger began to rise again. He missed Debbie and Ronnie immensely. His father? Not so much. And as he passed his father's old garage, Harvard Street Gulf, he thought about popcorn, car batteries, and blood—an odd confluence of subconscious thought, to be sure. But it all came together one particularly wild night.

Steve's father, Eddie, operated on the outer edges of the law—a little skimming off the top, a bit of loansharking, a touch of bookmaking, but no drugs. It turned out the heavyset man who owned the nearby newspaper stand owed Eddie about $2,000, but when the man came to the gas station late one night to pay up, the brown paper bag with a wad of cash in it was a little light.

"I can get the rest of it to you next week," the heavyset man said undaunted.

"All right, let's count it in back," Eddie said. "Away from the windows." Nothing to this point would indicate what was about to happen, but then Eddie turned to fourteen-year-old Steve and directed him to "Go get me a bag of popcorn."

Steve recognized the word "popcorn" as the code word his father had selected a long time ago. It meant that Steve was to lock the doors to the garage. Nobody was leaving. Suddenly, nineteen-year-old Ronnie Davis appeared from the office.

Despite being outweighed by over a hundred pounds, Eddie Davis attacked the man with a fury. It was not a wise decision. The man repeatedly blocked Eddie's blows with his shoulders and counterpunched him to the ground. Eddie was becoming a bloody mess, but he continued to get back up and absorb more punishment. As the two sons watched their father get beaten, there was a shared moment of joy. This three-hundred-pound man was doing what both of them had dreamed of doing so many times. But instead of thanking him, Ronnie climbed up on a desk, pulled down a car battery from a shelf, and slammed it on top of the man's head. Blood shot out like a geyser as the man stumbled across the garage floor and fell through a glass window.

The loud crash of shattering glass was followed by an inexplicable silence. No traffic went by. No distant sirens could be heard. The Davises didn't move. And the man was barely breathing.

"Did you kill him?" Steve whispered.

"I sure hope he didn't," Eddie said. "He still owes me a grand, plus the juice." Eddie quickly left the scene leaving Ronnie and Steve to clean up the blood with a few oily rags and an old mop. Once the evidence was washed away, Ronnie called for an ambulance, and the boys left before help arrived. Eddie was never questioned by police regarding the fat guy with the bashed in skull lying unconscious on his property. The police let it go the same way they let Eddie go the dozens of times they caught him driving drunk. It was a different time. How else to explain a father taking a boy out of school in the sixth grade to work full-time at a gas station as Eddie did with Steve?

John "Edward" Davis was an alcoholic, an abusive father and husband, and a child of some sickening abuse himself. Two of his brothers committed suicide. Paul hanged himself in a hotel room. Jimmy took a bottle of pills and left a note to his mother that read: "I'm doing this because of you. I hope you're happy now."

"My Dad had a rough upbringing," Davis acknowledges without sympathy. "Another one of his brothers was murdered in South Boston—gang-related. Robert was his name." Robert Davis had robbed a bank in the late 1950s and was waiting to stand trial. Coincidentally, a young Billy Bulger was hired to defend Robert Davis, but his case never made it to trial. Responding to a knock at his apartment door, Davis unsuspectingly opened the door and was blasted by a shotgun. He died with scars on his body, scars incurred when his mother had tied him to the furnace as a child.

These were the kinds of stories that were talked about openly in the Davis household. The family's history was splashed with tragedy, mystery, and a plethora of shady or outright illegal activity, but was otherwise typical.

Ed Davis married Olga Sciulli while the two were just teen-agers, on August 3, 1946. The marriage would produce ten children. Eileen, the oldest, was born when Olga was sixteen years old. After Eileen came Eddie Jr., Michael, Ronnie, Debbie, Steve, Sandy, Victor, Robbie, and Michelle. Despite the growing family and the decades together, it was not a happy marriage. Olga would say of her husband that he "paid the bills and kept the refrigerator full." She closed her eyes to the illegal and brutally violent activities taking place nightly at her husband's gas station, and paid no mind to the persistent abuse Edward inflicted on the boys, and less frequently, the girls. She also watched as eight of her ten children dropped out of school without a high school diploma.

"My father was very strict," Eileen understates, and then adds, "He was abusive. I don't know how abusive he was with my sisters. I'm another story. He beat me like I was Joe Frazier and he was Muhammad Ali one night." Eileen had committed the unforgivable sin of going to the movies with a group of friends, and Edward had gotten the idea that she was on a date. "I remember when my mother was carrying my brother, Victor," Eileen continues, "He hit her and kicked her in the pelvis. Ma had to stay in the hospital until the baby was born."

"I fuckin' hated him," Steve says flatly. "For dinner, he'd eat a big, fat steak, while we chewed on mayonnaise sandwiches. And in the morning we'd go to Martin's coffee shop up the street. He'd order me a milk and toast, and he'd get bacon and eggs. I wouldn't eat the toast. I despised him."

And that was long before Steve's most humiliating moment, the one that led him to seriously contemplate killing his father. He remembered standing at the foot of his father's bed, knife in hand, fury in his belly, and a mind just warped enough to convince him justice was waiting at the tip of a kitchen blade. Steve thought about the opportunity missed and felt both regret and relief.

It all started the day Debbie bounded happily into the house, which is something the Davis children tended not to do. They were usually only happy when they were leaving. And Debbie was leaving. "Tommy asked me to marry him," Debbie pronounced, and then preempting the obvious question from her parents, she added, "And no, I'm not pregnant." Debbie was barely sixteen years old when she and Tommy Latorneau decided their brief courtship had blossomed into true love. Debbie's adolescent presumption was that anything would be better than living at home. It wasn't. Not for her or for Steve. Tommy didn't often breathe without inhaling pot smoke. And when he regressed to an abusive alcoholic, Debbie was on familiar ground. She left Tommy while he was in jail and before their first anniversary.

During that same year, fifteen-year-old Steve also moved out of the house following a particularly wild night that left him bleeding and running barefoot through the snow. Eddie had come home from a local pub drunk again and angrier than usual. Shuffling unsteadily through the front door, he first spotted Steve at the kitchen table. Steve, whose hair was fashionably long in the early 1970s style, was immediately a target.

"You long haired faggot!" Eddie shouted. "You look like a girl."

Recognizing the potential this had for turning bad in a hurry, Steve tried to make his way up the stairs, but Eddie grabbed him hard by the arm.

"Olga! Bring me a dress!"

It was a strange demand, but Olga obliged. She grabbed the first one she could out of her closet and ran it down the stairs to Eddie.

"We lost a daughter when Debbie left. Now we got one back," Eddie announced. "Put this on!" He threw the dress at Steve who caught it, and threw it on the floor. "Put it on, or I'll put it on you!"

Olga pleaded with Eddie to stop, but he was enjoying himself too much to turn back now. Steve reluctantly, and with tears rolling down his cheeks, pulled the dress down over his head.

"Now twirl around a bit," Eddie ordered. "All you need is some lipstick and a ribbon in your hair and we got ourselves another little girl." Snickering to himself, Eddie labored up the stairs and collapsed on his bed.

Steve tore the dress off and ran out of the house. He collected himself and waited long enough for Eddie to pass out. When Steve returned to the house, he could hear the familiar sound of his father snoring. Steve took off his shoes and socks so as to be as quiet as possible. He grabbed the biggest knife he could find, passed his mother asleep on the couch, and crept up to his parent's room.

Standing there in the darkness, the knife by his side glimmering in the moonlight, Steve thought about the countless beatings he and his siblings had suffered, and the hatred for that mean drunk came rising back up like bile.

"He was on the bed just plopped on his back," Steve recalls. "I stood there with a big kitchen knife, and I was thinking of how to do it. I figure I'm gonna go right into his chest, but I gotta make sure it's gonna penetrate."

It's hard to say how long Steve stood there working up the courage to thrust the knife into his father's chest, but it was too long. The snoring suddenly stopped, and before Steve realized it, his father was sitting up and staring at him.

"You thinking of killing me?" Eddie asked without flinching. "You ain't got the balls, Mary."

Shaking with fear, Steve dropped the knife to the floor, and before the reverberations of the thud subsided, Eddie was on him. He started to beat Steve like he'd never done before with blows and solid punches to the face. A new level of cruelty was being delivered. The black-hearted father had flipped a switch from merciless to soulless.

"He startled me and I dropped the knife," Steve says regretfully. "He chased me around. He beat me real bad. He beat me like he was fighting a full-grown man."

But if Eddie's intention was to kill his son, he made an inauspicious miscalculation when he shoved Steve down the stairs. That was Steve's opportunity to get away. As Steve stumbled to the door, his father fired a solid gold cigarette lighter at him. It whizzed by Steve's cheek and buried itself in the wall.

"You could have killed him!" Olga shrieked.

Steve ran from the house, leaving a trail of blood in the snow. He was barefoot, but unaware of the cold, and he didn't stop running until he got to his brother Mickey's apartment. And he didn't return to his father's house until the next day when he knew Eddie was gone. Steve threw some of his clothes into a green trash bag, ripped off a stack of cash he had duct taped in aluminum foil to the underside of his dresser drawer, kissed his mother good-bye, and never slept another night under the same roof as his father. Their paths would cross from time to time, but the father-son relationship was dead long before Eddie was found floating in Marina Bay.

"We never found out what really killed my father," Eileen says. "I don't believe my father took a heart attack and drowned. I don't care how bad he was, he was still a human being."

Eddie Davis may have finally messed with the wrong guy— and the wrong car. Soon after Flemmi gave Debbie a 1974 two-door Jaguar XKE, Eddie took a sledgehammer to it. He dented the hood and the doors, took out the headlights, and smashed the windshield. It was Eddie's way of expressing his disapproval that his then eighteen-year-old divorced daughter was dating a much older, married mobster. Eddie Davis was not a decent man, but even he could see the wrong in that.

"If he wasn't your father, he'd be a dead man," Flemmi told Debbie. "I'd kill him for smashing up that car."

Four months later, Eddie Davis was found dead in Marina Bay. The police said he fell off his boat and drowned. His mother wouldn't permit an autopsy to be performed, and even though she had no authority to prevent it, nobody in the Davis family chose to fight her on it. So, it was never determined if alcohol had been a factor in Eddie Davis's death. After a day of fishing with a friend, there most certainly was alcohol in his system, but his boat was right next to the dock. Was he too drunk to swim a few feet?

"He was so bad to me and my brothers," Steve Davis says. "I went up to the coffin like it was sad. I was fake crying. I was more relieved the prick was gone. I always wanted a father image, but he was just a prick. No good."

Eddie Davis died much the same way he had lived: drunk, angry, and alone. Olga had left him after twenty-seven years of a bizarre, cruel, and unloving marriage. They were separated, but not divorced when Olga learned their home in Roslindale had burned to the ground. Nothing in the house was salvageable, including Eddie's things. He was at work at the time of the fire and, though police considered him a suspect, he was never charged. The family knows he put in an insurance claim, but no one knows what the settlement was. Olga and the kids didn't ask questions.

"He did it," Steve accuses. "Gas and a match. He did it because he and my mother separated. She was leaving him. He burned it down just so she couldn't have it. She wouldn't have him. She wouldn't have anything."

So, Edward Davis was out of the picture in 1975. His death ruled an accident. He was a drowning victim. The police had no reason to suspect foul play, but Steve did.

"Flemmi knew my father was going to be trouble for him," Steve says. "Now or later. He was a time bomb. He didn't like Flemmi dating my sister. Not one bit."

Suspicions only grew as the Davis family dwindled. Ronnie was eventually killed in prison. Then Debbie disappeared, and Michelle, the youngest of the Davis children, died after making a startlingly horrific revelation. There were simply too many connections, too much coincidence to be ignored. Steve Flemmi and Whitey Bulger were destroying the Davis family one by one.

CHAPTER TWO

Beauty and the Beast

A few days after Steve Davis's audience with Bulger, his brother, Mickey, was badly beaten. And as Steve looked at his brother's swollen face, he put himself back in the room with Bulger and thought, *I could have killed the son of a bitch. The other two would be thinking he killed me, and then I could have taken them both out as they came racing up the stairs. Three dead assholes. Easy as that. And the world would be a better place for it. If I'd brought in my gun, I would have killed Whitey Bulger, and that fuckhead Flemmi, too.*

Justice with the touch of a trigger.

Instead, Bulger and Flemmi lived, and his sister was murdered by two gangsters protected by the FBI, her body contemptuously discarded into a marshy area of the Neponset River in Quincy where it lay undiscovered for nearly twenty years. And all along Davis knew Flemmi had something to do with it. "I assumed it from the beginning that he killed her," Steve acknowledges. "But even a thug has hopes. I had hope.

So, maybe for a while I thought she might have run off, because she might have thought that was her only way out. In my mind, in my heart, I was waiting to hear the good news. Maybe she was slick enough to get away. She's in Mexico maybe. But I'm from the street. And I knew Flemmi wasn't putting enough effort into looking for her. Turns out she let her guard down. I thought she was a little sharper than that."

Debbie Davis's guard was down from the moment Steve Flemmi walked into George Taylor's jewelry store in Brookline. The year was 1972. Debbie was working behind the counter when she noticed the husky, dark-haired man wearing sunglasses walk in. He had a pointed nose with big nostrils, and a thick neck—not particularly handsome, but he smelled nice, wore fine jewelry, and exuded a sense of importance that could be considered impressive. Debbie had long, wavy, dirty blonde hair that had inspired comparisons to a young Farrah Fawcett. Young indeed. Debbie had just turned seventeen. Flemmi was forty-three. And both of them were in what you might call complicated relationships.

Debbie, who had been working at the jewelry store for about a year after dropping out of high school, was still married to Tommy Latorneau, but it hadn't taken long for his alcoholism to exact a toll on the marriage, and the young lovers were in the process of getting a divorce. Flemmi helped expedite the divorce by paying for Debbie's attorney. Flemmi, not only remained married, he also took on a common law wife, all while embarking on a sexual relationship with Debbie.

First, there was Jeannette. Flemmi met her soon after returning from decorated service in the Korean War. That's where his expert marksmanship earned him his nickname, "The Rifleman." He married Jeannette on March 17, 1956. Within a few years, Flemmi was deep into criminal behavior and adulterous philandering. He began a longstanding sexual relationship with a woman named Marion Hussey in 1959.

It turns out Marion was also married, but she was estranged from her husband, Tom, when she started up with Flemmi. They met while she was tending bar, and after sleeping together for a short time, she graciously accepted Flemmi's offer to move her and her daughter Deborah to a nicer apartment on Norton Street in Dorchester, and then Westfield Street. Flemmi spent five nights a week with them, played the role of husband and father, bought toys for Deborah, and jewelry and cars for Marion, all while still married to Jeannette, who he found out, was the jealous type.

Jeanette finally discovered the truth about her husband's infidelity. So, one day when she was out driving, she spotted Flemmi and Marion in a car together. She simply put her foot on the gas and smashed her car right into them. Flemmi and Jeannette separated after that, but they never divorced.

Marion and Tom Hussey would also remain married while Marion gave birth to three of Flemmi's children: William, Stephanie, and Stephen—all given the last name Hussey, rather than Flemmi. In fact, Marion was pregnant with William while she sat with Flemmi in the car that Jeannette rammed from behind.

So, when Flemmi walked into the jewelry store that day, he could have been shopping for Jeanette, or Marion, or perhaps one of the other young girls he enjoyed on the side. Flemmi was a player and a gangster, and Debbie Davis was immediately smitten.

"What's a beautiful young girl like you working in a place like this?" Flemmi said as if he were the first.

And to be sure, Debbie Davis was a beautiful young girl. It was a long time in the making, however. She had been a chubby child and was partially disfigured when she was five years old. She and Steve, who was closest to her in age and in relationship, were bouncing on her bed. Their giggles echoed through the house until they were interrupted by a sickening, dull thud. Both children were motionless. Steve was frozen by fear. Debbie was momentarily unconscious as a small pool of blood formed around her head.

"Maaaaa!" Steve finally managed to yell.

By the time Olga reached the bedroom, Debbie was sitting up and crying. Her right eye had already begun to swell. Olga heard the story through blubbering tears that Steve had come down on the bed just as Debbie was jumping up. The sudden extra force sent Debbie flying off the bed as if jettisoned by a trampoline. Her eye hit the corner of the radiator, and she would remain cross-eyed for many years. Of course, when Eddie heard the story, he whipped Steve on his bare bottom with a metal spatula.

Debbie's vision impairment was never addressed surgically. There was no money for such things, and since it didn't affect Debbie's ability to read or learn, her parents saw no urgency. It wasn't until she was a teenager that Debbie's lowering self-esteem inspired her to wear corrective lenses, and the problem disappeared. That is to say, she was no longer cross-eyed the day she met Steve Flemmi, but her low self-image may have contributed to her generous responses to Flemmi's sexual advances. There were undoubtedly other factors as well.

"We're in a different time zone now," Steve Davis tries to explain. "When you have nothing—it's like when a guy has a nice car, he gets all the girls. We didn't get nothing from our father. We got beaten. We never got any gifts or anything. Everybody wants more. So, she was sucked in by being a kid with nothing."

By the time Flemmi left the jewelry store that day, Debbie had agreed to let him take her out to dinner. She ignored the admonitions of her little brother, Steve, who told her Flemmi was a "bad guy." He didn't seem like a bad guy when he took her to Chandlers in South Boston, or for Japanese food at a little place in Somerville. None of the so-called good guys she'd dated up to that point had ever treated her so well.

"Besides," Debbie asked with a naiveté that belied her upbringing, but bespoke her youth, "What's he gonna do to me?" Perhaps, it was an indication that she really didn't care what he did to her, or she gravely underestimated Flemmi's potential for evil.

Additionally, she disregarded her mother's pronouncement that Flemmi "is some kind of a bookmaker." Why Olga would minimize what she knew of Flemmi is unclear. Certainly, Olga would have known that Flemmi, her childhood acquaintance, was also by then one of the leaders of the Winter Hill Gang, a clandestine criminal organization. She must also have known that Flemmi was friends with Whitey Bulger. After all, who didn't know that? And that Bulger had already served nine years in prison for robbing banks, and had a reputation for extreme violence.

Olga may even have known, as many people did, that Flemmi was at a Roxbury bar on May 4, 1964, when his friend and mentor Edward "Wimpy" Bennett killed Frank Benjamin. Flemmi apparently had so much difficulty cleaning up the blood, as he would later testify, he set fire to the bar.

Wimpy and his brother, Walter Bennett, were loansharks who worked with Flemmi out of a bar called Walter's Lounge on Dudley Street. A third Bennett brother, William, tended bar there. In January 1967, a confrontation about some missing money ended with Flemmi killing Wimpy by shooting him in the head. Later that year, as part of a growing turf war, Walter Bennett was strangled, and William was shot and thrown from a car in Dorchester. William's body was found in a snowbank two days before Christmas in 1967.

Undoubtedly, Olga and the entire Davis family would have been aware that Flemmi and another reputed mobster, Frank Salemme, were indicted for William's murder. This was commonly known and all over the newspapers.

"I don't read newspapers," Olga had claimed when asked later in court. "I don't like them in the house." And why, under oath and challenged about her supposed lack of knowledge of Flemmi's crimes, would she later claim not to like newspapers in her house? "They draw bugs," she said flatly.

Even without the benefit of media reports, it can be assumed that rumors from the street filtered into the Davis household. Knowing Flemmi had been indicted for the murder of William Bennett, it might be natural to wonder if Flemmi were also involved in the disappearances of his brothers, Edward and Walter, who hadn't been seen since January 18 and March 6 of 1967, respectively. Their bodies have never been found. Salemme would later tell police he and Flemmi buried the bodies outside the Hopkinton's Sportsmen's Club, but it's presumed the bodies were inadvertently moved during the Big Dig, a $15 billion public works project that relocated millions of tons of dirt from downtown Boston.

Olga could also have explained to her seventeen-year-old daughter that the man she was so excited to be going out with was at that time a fugitive from justice. The indictment against Flemmi for William Bennett's murder came down on September 11, 1969. A few weeks later, he was also indicted for the attempted murder of a lawyer named John Fitzgerald on January 30, 1968.

"The bomb was placed under the hood of attorney Fitzgerald's car in Everett next to his office," Flemmi would later explain. "He got in the car, and the car exploded, and he got injured."

Fitzgerald lost his left leg and his right leg below the knee. He'd had the misfortune of becoming hitman Joey Barboza's attorney, a circumstance that worsened when Barboza agreed to testify against the Raymond Patriarca crime family, a ruthless mob organization based out of Providence, Rhode Island.

Barboza, nicknamed "The Animal" and described by the FBI as the "most vicious criminal in New England," had first agreed to accept $50,000 from the mob not to testify, but reneged on the deal. The presumption by the mob was that Fitzgerald convinced Barboza to change his mind. Thus, the car bomb.

But, it would be discovered later that it was actually Steve Flemmi who, in his role as a top echelon informant for the FBI, got Barboza to testify, not Fitzgerald. In essence, Flemmi bombed Fitzgerald's car, maiming him for life, for something Flemmi was actually guilty of.

But Flemmi had friends in high places. FBI Special Agent Paul Rico tipped Flemmi off about the impending criminal indictments, which allowed Flemmi to skip town with Salemme and another man, Peter Poulos. Poulos was there when Flemmi killed Wimpy Bennett, and may have helped in the murder of William Bennett. Now, according to Rico, Poulos had been in contact with law enforcement about possibly cutting a deal. As an informant himself, Flemmi couldn't risk Poulos becoming one, too. Poulos's days were numbered.

On September 11, 1969, the day of the first indictment, Poulos's mother had several conversations with a man named "Steve," (presumably Flemmi), who was urgently trying to reach Poulos. When Poulos finally came home, he called Steve, and soon after he hung up the phone, he packed a few clothes, grabbed $50,000, and told his mother he was going on a vacation to Cape Cod.

The three fugitives, Salemme, Flemmi, and Poulos went to California to hide out instead. Soon after they arrived, a Mafia associate named Phil Waggenheim brought out a gun to Flemmi to use to kill Poulos. Salemme went to New York while Flemmi and Poulos drove toward Las Vegas. At some point during their trip through the desert, Flemmi said to Poulos, "Let's change seats." When they stopped and got out of the car, Flemmi shot Poulos once in the head and once in the chest. Poulos's body would be found by employees of the Nevada Highway Department in Clark County. The crew had been picking up trash.

Flemmi met up with Salemme in New York where the two had a falling out. Salemme assumed a superior role in the relationship, and Flemmi didn't like it. Flemmi left for Canada and told Rico where Salemme was hiding out. Salemme was arrested and spent sixteen years in jail.

The bond between Rico and Flemmi was strong. It dated back several years, and it would continue for several decades. As far back as 1965, Rico knew that Flemmi was a killer and did nothing about it. Flemmi's first murder may have been Edward "Punchy" McLaughlin, a former boxer and enforcer for his brothers' gang in Charlestown. Punchy had shot Flemmi's brother, Jimmy, who survived the shooting. So, when Punchy got off the bus in front of the John J. Moakley United States Courthouse in Boston, Flemmi stepped out from the side of the building and shot and killed him.

"Nice shooting," Rico later complimented Flemmi.

While Flemmi was hiding from the feds, there were occasions when Rico would indicate to Flemmi that it was safe to come back to the United States for a short time. Those were the times when Marion Hussey would bring the four children down to New York for a visit, or Flemmi would venture into Boston to take care of some business before going back into hiding. Marion maintained that while she knew Flemmi was on the run, she didn't know what the charges were against him. "Because we never discussed it," she'd say. Marion simply left her trysts with Flemmi, and returned to the home he had bought for her just prior to becoming a fugitive. It was a large house located at 1046 Blue Hill Avenue in Milton, a suburb just outside Boston. The house originally had seven rooms, but several additions later, it was a fifteen-room mansion with an apartment over a two-car garage, a swimming pool, cabana, and tennis court. It was a great place to throw a "welcome home party," which Flemmi did in May 1974.

That's when Rico gave Flemmi the greenlight to come back home. He not only told him it was safe, he made a veiled threat to Flemmi effectively telling him he had better come home. Rico needed Flemmi's help to take down the Boston Mafia. He saw to it that the charges against Flemmi were dropped.

It was now safe for Flemmi to pick up where he had left off, but things were even better now. Winter Hill had won the gang war while Flemmi was away. There was a lot of money being made in drugs, loansharking, and shaking down bookies. "There was a gang war in Boston," long-time bookie and Quincy High School graduate Dickie O'Brien says. "People were shot, and Mr. Bulger ended up on top. So, you can draw your own conclusions." The only reasonable conclusion is that Bulger, Howie Winter, John Martorano, and eventually Flemmi had shot, killed, stabbed, and beaten their way to the top of organized crime in Boston, and their reign of terror lasted three decades. "In those days," another bookie James Katz says, "it was murders and a lot of beatings. Was I afraid of Mr. Bulger? Absolutely." Dickie O'Brien also feared for his life while running numbers and football cards from 1971 until he retired and left the business to his daughter in 1993. For fourteen of those years, he paid Bulger and Flemmi anywhere from $200 to $2,000 a month—rent they called it, but it was extortion. He also once paid $60,000 when Winter Hill forced him to take on someone else's bad debt. "I valued my own life as well as those with me," is how O'Brien explained why he paid the rent.

He knew what the penalty was for failing to pay. He heard it right from Bulger's own mouth, and he believed it. An unlucky gambler, George Labate, was one of O'Brien's two dozen or so agents—guys who worked the street collecting bets. If the agents won money, they got 10 percent of the profit. If they lost money, they owed the entire amount lost. Labate owed O'Brien several thousand dollars, but was making no effort to pay. He even stopped returning phone calls. When Bulger found out, he found Labate at a bar.

"Were you treated right by Dickie O'Brien?" Bulger asked.

"Yes, I was," Labate answered nervously.

"Then what are you doing?"

Bulger let Labate explain that he was going to pay O'Brien as soon as he got his own new business up and running. Labate had big plans and was getting out of the business.

"You know, we have a business besides bookmaking, too," Bulger told him.

"Oh, yeah? What's that?"

"Killing assholes like you."

Bulger laughed whenever he heard that story, and his grin lingered as he recalled that Labate paid up. Everybody did. O'Brien says he regularly made his payments by bringing a paper bag full of cash to Triple O's or to the Lancaster Street garage. He'd put the money on a table and walk away. He says Bulger never grabbed the money. It was always Flemmi who reached for it.

At the end of his workdays, Flemmi went home to Milton where he subjected Marion to a steady assault of physical and verbal abuse. He also began sexually abusing Deborah when she was sixteen years old. Deborah was not Flemmi's daughter by blood, but Stephanie was, and he began having sex with her some years later when she was sixteen. The sordid details of his depravity were first exposed in October 1984.

It was a typically brisk autumn day in New England when Marion returned home to the sounds of Flemmi and her daughter Deborah arguing upstairs. Even though Deborah no longer lived at the house, seeing her there or hearing her argue with Flemmi was not at all uncommon. Marion, not especially concerned at first, brought her purse to the kitchen and dropped her keys on the table. She stood for a moment and looked over the property. The leaves were a beautiful bouquet of bright oranges and reds. She soaked it in for a moment, inhaled deeply, reminded herself to hire someone to sweep the fallen leaves off the tennis court and determinedly started up the stairs. "More of the same," she thought, but she couldn't have been more wrong.

The argument between Flemmi and Deborah was indecipherable at first. Marion could make out some key words, such as "drugs" and "whore" and "Jaguar I bought you!" Nothing new there. Now twenty-four years old, Deborah was a part-time prostitute and full-time drug addict. She had dropped out of Quincy College and began waiting tables at a bar in what was then known as the Combat Zone in Boston. Drugs and prostitution were on every street corner, and Deborah was doing both. She also had part-time jobs as a stripper and a thief. And she was a full-time pain in Flemmi's ass.

"I won't let you touch me anymore!" Deborah yelled loudly and clearly, and it was enough to freeze Marion in the hallway. When Marion finally moved again, it was backward and down the stairs. This had the potential of turning into something she couldn't face. She'd seen the signs, and either willfully ignored them, or stupidly didn't recognize them as such. But she had noticed Deborah flinch when Flemmi touched her or walked by too closely. She watched Deborah grow more distant, and sensed the tension between them. Deborah had gone from being a good kid to a rebellious, disobedient drug user almost as soon as Flemmi re-entered the family dynamic.

Marion would have kept retreating down the stairs, but she heard the sounds of slapping and crying. So, in a rare moment of courage, she marched up the stairs to defend her daughter, quite possibly for the first time. "What the hell is going on in here?" Marion shouted as she swung open Deborah's bedroom door. And before she could utter another word, she gasped at what she saw. There was Deborah, shirt open, no bra. She had her hands in front of her tear-stained face as Flemmi swung at her forcefully with open palms.

"Ma! Help me!" she cried.

Flemmi stopped and turned around. Marion gave him a look that was equal parts confusion and disapproval. She didn't like that he was hitting her daughter, but more to the point, she didn't know why he was doing it, or why Deborah was half naked on the bed.

"Stevie, honey," she said. "You need to take her out of here. Debbie, put some clothes on and go with your father. We'll sort all this out later."

Then Deborah hit her mother with the bomb that had been ticking down toward detonation for the better part of a decade. "He makes me suck his prick! I hate him! I've been doing it for years!" Deborah waited for some kind of a response to her dramatic proclamation, but the room went silent. Flemmi's knees buckled, and his heart felt something that might actually have been guilt. But he couldn't speak. Marion stared first at Deborah, but not with any discernible sympathy or compassion. No, what Deborah saw in her mother's eyes was regret. Marion knew in an instant what price had been paid for their luxurious lifestyle, and who it was that had paid most dearly for it. It wasn't worth it. This was her fault. And she hated herself for it.

So, Marion looked over at Flemmi. His eyes revealed himself like they had never done before. She knew in that instant what a monster he truly was. He just wasn't worth it. This was his fault. And she hated him for it. Without a word, Marion left the room. She didn't run over and hug her battered child. She offered no tender words of healing. Instead, she acted as few other mothers would—she left an abusive monster alone with her daughter.

"Ma!" Deborah shouted. "I'm not lying!"

Marion hesitated briefly before continuing a hurried walk down the stairs. Flemmi stayed in the bedroom, and while Deborah got fully dressed, he threw some of her clothes into a suitcase.

"Debbie, I believe you," was all Marion said as Flemmi led Deborah toward the front door. Deborah wiped tears from her eyes and showed her mother a look that may have been gratitude. There was at least some comfort in being believed. There was a long embrace between the two women. As they held on to each other, they tried to let go of the past. So much anger and resentment had built up between them. Flemmi stood by discomfited as if he were a scolded child who didn't know if he were allowed to speak or even move. When Deborah broke from her mother, she brushed quickly past Flemmi who followed her out to the car.

Even after all this, Marion allowed Flemmi to drive off with her daughter and return her to an apartment in the Back Bay where so much of the abuse had occurred. It's difficult to find a suitable explanation for the way Marion behaved on this night.

When Flemmi came back to the house the next day, Marion screamed and threatened and cried hysterically. She even broke a few things, and ultimately threw Flemmi out of the house, saying, "I want all your stuff out of here by tomorrow!" Anything of his that remained in the Blue Hill Avenue mansion the next day, Marion threw away. But the relationship didn't really end there. Despite what she knew for a fact, and despite the rumors she heard and believed to be true—that Flemmi had sexual relationships with many other teenage girls, including several sisters of one South Boston family—she allowed Flemmi to move back in with her about a year later.

This would be after Flemmi had watched Whitey Bulger kill her daughter, and after Flemmi had ripped Deborah's teeth out with pliers, and after he had helped dispose of her body near Florian Hall in Dorchester.

Marion, of course, didn't know those things at the time. And when she welcomed Flemmi back home, Marion still didn't know that he had also sexually abused her other daughter, Stephanie.

Deborah had kept silent while she withstood a decade of abuse. Stephanie kept silent, too, and Marion kept the dark secret to herself. She never told anyone of Flemmi's sexual interactions with his daughters. She didn't report it the police, claiming that she couldn't trust any of them, because they were on Flemmi's payroll. And not only did she never speak to Deborah or Stephanie about it again, she sat idly by while Deborah vanished from her life. She thought Deborah had gone to live in California or Ohio, or maybe Florida for a while. She remembers getting a Mother's Day card once, but couldn't be sure from where it was mailed. In fact, the last time she ever saw Deborah was shortly after the sexual abuse revelation when they went apple picking together.

Deborah had stayed out of touch for long periods of time before, so it took a few months before Marion started to wonder what happened to her. In the early part of 1985, she asked a Massachusetts State Police Officer, Joseph Saccardo, to help locate her. Marion had first met Saccardo nearly twenty years earlier when he rushed her to the hospital in the back of his police car to give birth to her son, Stephen.

Saccardo began by asking people in the South Shore area when they had last seen Deborah, or if they had any information as to her whereabouts. He found no leads, but was told by other officers that some "serious people were pissed off that he was making an inquiry." Saccardo assumed it was Bulger and Flemmi, and after failing to find Deborah, he eventually presumed she was dead. He never told Marion about his theory. So, she continued to believe Deborah was alive. Eventually, she gave up hope and came to the conclusion that Deborah was dead, but she would claim never to even consider that Deborah had been killed, or that Flemmi may have killed her. Despite knowing what a bad guy Flemmi was, Marion may reasonably have thought, "Even he wouldn't murder his own daughter." She was wrong.

Marion was as wrong as the Davis family, who knew their Debbie went missing in 1981 just as her relationship with the thug was going sour, yet they failed to get answers or to even distance themselves from Flemmi. The smartest thing might have been to completely shut Flemmi out of their lives, but they didn't. Olga simply said "thank you" when Flemmi gave her a Cadillac Eldorado.

"It wasn't a new one," she would say, "But it was well kept."

Of course, the Davis family immediately suspected Flemmi was involved in Debbie's disappearance, as unlike Deborah Hussey, Debbie Davis had never gone missing before. She spoke to her mother several times a day, until the day it suddenly stopped. So, when Debbie was gone, the immediate assumption was that she was dead. Hope prevented that from being a certainty, but it was most assuredly the prevailing thought at the time.

"He knew he was losing her," Debbie's brother Victor told the *Boston Globe* in 1998, referring to the deteriorating relationship of Flemmi and Debbie. "And on top of that, he thought she may have known a little bit too much about his relationship with the Feds." Victor told the newspaper that the family "immediately suspected Flemmi had killed her." Olga herself was quoted in the *Boston Herald* around the same time. She said, "Sometimes I would like to take that Steve Flemmi by the shoulders and shake him until he tells me." Olga also told the *South Coast Today* that she thought Flemmi might have been involved in her daughter's death, but she kept quiet "for fear that Flemmi or his associates might harm her remaining seven children." And she told the *Patriot Ledger* in 2000 that she invited Flemmi to her son Steve's wedding a year after Debbie went missing just "to keep the peace."

Olga recanted that story in a deposition a few years later. When the attorney read excerpts from those articles, she said,

"That's a lie. It's a lie. I never said something like that. That's why we invited him to the wedding, to keep peace? Come on, will you."

Without proof, without so much as a body, and certainly without any help from the police or FBI, there wasn't much the Davis family could do about Flemmi—other than to stay as far away from him as possible. They chose not to.

An FBI report from November 1, 1983, noted that: "The Mickey Davis operation pays tribute—money—to Stephen Flemmi, a known Winter Hill Gang member, at a rate of approximately two-thousand dollars per week for protection and territorial rights for distribution of cocaine in the Medford, Malden, Revere and Somerville areas."

That same report accused the other Davis brothers, Eddie, Steve, and Victor, of "operating both together and independently various cocaine and marijuana distribution networks in the Boston area," and that "one of the focal points of their organization is located at the residence of their mother, Olga Davis, in Randolph, Massachusetts." This report went on to say, "Eddie Davis brings large quantities of marijuana to his brother Victor at an address in Randolph, MA. Eddie Davis's organization is also paying Steve Flemmi for protection and territorial rights." Additionally, the FBI bugged Olga's phone at 17 Burris Way in Randolph, and claimed the wiretaps along with an unidentified source produced incriminating information against her son Steve Davis:

The source stated that someone has recently opened a sub shop in Fields Corner, Dorchester, and is pushing cocaine and marijuana for Stevie Davis from that shop. Source advises Stevie Davis has been bragging about his activities with Steve Flemmi. Source advised Stevie Davis and

Flemmi are getting closer, but does not know what's going on between them. . . . Recently, Stevie Davis and Eddie Davis were given the okay by Steve Flemmi to deal drugs, cocaine and marijuana.

It was also conjectured that when Eddie had gone to jail a few years prior to 1983 for the theft of fur coats that he had sold them to Flemmi.

Olga would deny any knowledge of this, but did acknowledge that Flemmi was still coming around to see her in Randolph two or three times a week in 1983. That's two years after Debbie disappeared, two years after Olga thought Flemmi probably killed her daughter, and about eighteen months after she allowed Flemmi, then fifty-two, to show an unnatural interest in her youngest daughter, Michelle, who was sixteen at the time. Whatever her reasons were, Olga remained friendly with Flemmi and maintained an inexplicable trust in him. In her deposition, Olga explained it this way: "Michelle was living with me. He did that while she was living with me—got her a car, got her clothes. I thought he was being nice, knowing I didn't have that kind of money. I had one income, and I thought he was, you know, trying to help out."

A mere six months after Debbie went missing, Flemmi began taking young Michelle out to dinner. Olga didn't presume anything nefarious was happening "because he would bring her right back home." Michelle had a different take on the situation. "My sister was gone, and he was her boyfriend, and he's trying to be with me," Michelle told the *Herald American* in a January 2000 interview. "It didn't make sense. Didn't he love my sister? Why would he be touching me and buying me things when my sister was missing?"

Years later, Michelle was changing her son Charles' diapers when Olga broke a lifelong tradition of not asking questions for which she was afraid of the answers. "Yes, mama," Michelle answered calmly. Then the river of emotions that had been dammed up for nearly twenty years came rushing through, and she wailed, "He's an *animal!*"

Flemmi had sexually abused Michelle when she was between the ages of sixteen and twenty-five. Flemmi's lust had taken him from Debbie Davis to Deborah Hussey on to Michelle Davis and back to his own biological daughter, Stephanie. Each girl was sixteen or seventeen when the sexual abuse began, and twenty-five or twenty-six when they were discarded, either by murder or by callous indifference.

Olga cried with her daughter. She thought back about all the things Flemmi had bought for them—clothes, cars, tuition, and dinners. She thought about how he had comforted her when Debbie went missing and had helped with the bills from time to time. "I thought he was being nice," Olga had told herself all along.

Michelle, however, knew firsthand the horrible truth. "He's a pedophile," she told the *Herald* in 2000. "That's his M.O. He goes after little girls and buys them things. I'm a victim. I'm grateful to be alive." In a lawsuit filed in 2001, Michelle claimed something the other girls did not—that Flemmi had beaten her over a period of nine years, and that she "lived in great fear of Stephen J. Flemmi."

Some people might say Olga Davis and Marion Hussey were at the very least guilty of willful ignorance in terms of not protecting their daughters from Flemmi. Others may cast judgment on both women far more harshly. Intentional blindness is not a mother's defense.

When the Davis, Hussey, and Litif families filed a wrongful death lawsuit in July 2009, they alleged the FBI was liable in the deaths of their family members, because it should have foreseen the murders. U.S. Attorney Lawrence Eiser told the court:

> Marion Hussey is going to say "I had no idea." She'll say "I had no idea that my daughter was in danger of being killed by Stephen Flemmi. The FBI should have known, but I didn't know." Even though, and she'll testify, Flemmi molested both of her daughters, involved both of her sons in crime, supported her for over some thirty years in a mansion, a twenty room mansion with a pool, tennis court, cabana. That's all blood money coming to her from Flemmi from his life of crime, and she comes in here and says, "It's not my fault." She protected, nurtured—she washed his clothes after he cut the teeth out of all these people. And she's going to blame the FBI? She's not his victim. She's his accomplice.

It was a losing argument for Eiser to suggest anyone, especially a mother, was an accomplice to a murder she couldn't even have anticipated. Despite Marion Hussey's firsthand knowledge of Flemmi's predilection for young girls, including his own daughters, she had hoped he cared for them in his own way. He had certainly demonstrated this with Deborah by getting her out of trouble when she went drinking at Triple O's, or committed robberies, or turned tricks in the Combat Zone. He'd see to it that she wasn't arrested by putting a call into his brother, Michael, who was, conveniently enough, a crooked cop. More than once Flemmi had gotten up in the middle of the night, grabbed a pistol, and pulled Deborah out of a dangerous situation. He even paid $4,000 to send her to

a drug rehab program to straighten her out, but she fell back
into her patterns of behavior. Eiser speculated in court that
Flemmi killed Deborah for two reasons: first, to hide his sexual
relationship with her, and second because he disapproved of
her lifestyle.

For Deborah Hussey and Debbie Davis the end would
come quickly and suddenly—and unsuspectingly. Each would
be lured by Flemmi into a home where Whitey Bulger was
waiting to pounce. With the premeditation of a coward, Bulger
attacked from behind and strangled the young women until he
successfully took their lives.

Michelle Davis, most likely haunted by the memories
and untreated trauma of Flemmi's abuse, became addicted to
heroin, cocaine, and alcohol. She died of a drug overdose in
2006. Similarly, Stephanie Hussey's drug and alcohol abuse
led directly to her death in 1999. She died of liver disease at
the age of thirty-eight. On her deathbed, she put pen to paper
and described Flemmi as the predator and abuser that he was.
Flemmi may not have strangled Debbie or Deborah, or forced
Michelle or Stephanie into drug addiction, but he is certainly
culpable in their deaths.

CHAPTER THREE

The Summer of 1981

With her right hand loosely gripping the fine leather steering wheel of a brand new Mercedes convertible, and her left hand pushing her long, thick blonde hair off her tanned face, Debbie Davis made the familiar turn into Presidential Acres in West Randolph. It was the summer of 1981 and Debbie's head rocked to the rhythm of Joan Jett's "I Love Rock 'n' Roll" blaring from the car speakers.

The music stopped abruptly as she hurriedly parked the car and turned off the engine. Gathering her things, she paused to look out across the neighboring highway. The rancid smell of the expansive town dump had caught her attention. She could see what seemed like hundreds of seagulls swooping amid the large piles of garbage. Sometimes she could ignore their squawking and the thought of them fighting each other for scraps, and instead convinced herself there was a graceful beauty to their fanciful flight. Such was the case today. So, Debbie smiled. It was an odd juxtaposition: a vibrant young woman with Hollywood beauty, bejeweled with diamonds, sitting in an expensive car looking out over a landfill and smiling joyfully. But in truth, Debbie's entire adult life had been a strange cross-section of high class and low class.

For nearly a decade, Debbie had been Steve Flemmi's on-again, off-again girlfriend. During that time she wore opulent jewelry, spent thousands of dollars on an elaborate wardrobe, and drove a series of luxury automobiles. Her first car was the Jaguar her father destroyed, then she accidentally wrecked a Datsun 240Z and a Corvette. Debbie was not a good driver. Perhaps, that was a family trait. When Steve Davis was fifteen years old, he crashed a Chevrolet Impala into a car full of nuns—three to be exact. The nuns were fine, and Steve went on to have several more accidents. Sometimes he reported the damaged car stolen, and if the insurance money was more than he paid for the car, he took that. He even had a friend blow up one of his cars with a Molotov cocktail, because the Blue Book value he'd receive from the insurance company was more than he had paid for it.

As for Debbie, she always looked like a million bucks, even though she routinely had barely enough money for gas. "Gotta run in and get some cash," Debbie would tell her cousin Donna as they pulled up to the Marconi Club.

Flemmi was her own personal ATM and she'd usually find him in the club sitting at his favorite table. When he wanted to feel like a big shot, he'd peel off a couple of hundred dollar bills and tuck the money in Debbie's shirt. But if he wanted to exert a bit more control, he'd give her a few singles, frequently leaving her to bum gas money from friends and family. "Everybody thought Steve gave her a lot of money," Eileen explains, "But he would only give her five to ten dollars, and part of that money had to be used to buy him a can of tuna fish."

And in 1981, there was definitely something fishy about Debbie's extreme drop in elevation. After spending a few years living in the penthouse of a high-rise community at 5060 Longwood Avenue in affluent Brookline, Massachusetts, Debbie was now making her home in blue-collar West Randolph in a modest apartment building with just four lanes of highway separating it from a dump. And it was on the first floor, which as any gangster knows, is not a smart idea.

"When you rent, you rent high," Steve Davis explains. "It gives you more time to do anything you need to do, to hide a gun, or to get away. This prick, Flemmi, was planning this. You don't put your girl in a ground level apartment across from the town dump." Getting inside the mind of a gangster is a dangerous and inexact proposition. Debbie had learned that much. Her brother, Steve though, thought like a criminal, because he was one. He hid his money, carried a gun, looked over his shoulder as he walked down the street, sat in public with his back to the wall, and spent a lot of time deliberating over "what if" scenarios. And when he saw Flemmi put his sister in a first floor apartment, he knew Flemmi didn't plan on spending a lot of time there. What if the cops or an enemy showed up? "Being a thug, you're not gonna put yourself there," Davis continues. "Him, as paranoid as he is, he wouldn't do that."

So, Steve assumed the move downward was a precursor to Flemmi finally and irrevocably severing his relationship with Debbie. He knew the abuse had been going on for years. He was there the day his brother, Ronnie, flicked a cigarette in Flemmi's face. Flemmi had slapped Debbie, and then came looking for her at Eddie Davis's garage. Debbie did, in fact, go there to cry on her brothers' shoulders, but she was gone by the time Flemmi arrived. Only Steve and Ronnie were there to greet Flemmi.

"Why would you do that?" Steve asked. "What could she have possibly done to deserve that?

Ronnie was less inquisitive. He impulsively flicked his cigarette at Flemmi hitting him in the right eye. Before the sparks hit the ground, Ronnie was in Flemmi's face. "If you ever do that again," Ronnie shouted. "I'll fucking kill you! I'll put a bullet in you. You hear me? You ever lay another hand on her, I will kill you."

Flemmi left without leaving much of an impression on the Davis boys. They no longer thought of him as the killer he was rumored to be. To them, Flemmi was just a gutless punk. They were wrong.

By 1981 Flemmi's violent outbursts against Debbie were increasing both in number and intensity. Before the relocation to Randolph, there was an altercation at Olga's house when Flemmi ended an argument with Debbie by slapping her across the face. Knowing about the abuse and seeing it firsthand elicited very different responses, and Mickey Davis reacted by jumping to his sister's defense. He grabbed Flemmi by the shirt and warned him never to hit his sister again. Mickey was barely 5'7" and didn't present much of a physically intimidating presence, but Flemmi offered no resistance.

Then after the move to Presidential Acres, Debbie went so far as to call the police. When Randolph detective John Henault arrived at the apartment, he shared a brief moment of recognition with Debbie. This wasn't the first time the two had met. Debbie had called Henault in the past to tell him that she knew Flemmi was involved in a few jewelry heists, and, yes, even murder. She didn't have any proof of those crimes, but on the night of the 9-1-1 call, the bruising under her eye and the puffiness of her cheek proved she'd been struck by Flemmi again. But Debbie didn't press charges. Henault, perhaps relieved that he didn't have to arrest Flemmi, simply escorted him out of the apartment, and another domestic abuse case was closed.

The arguing. The hitting. The apologizing. The resolution. It had all been played out so many times before. It was good theater, mostly harmless, and with a familiar ending. There was occasional comfort in that. Getting knocked down wasn't so bad when you got up and drove away in a Mercedes. Debbie put up with the bad, because the good was pretty great.

Debbie only knew of two worlds: the one with Flemmi and the one without. Her old life, certainly no safer than this one, was a half-step up from poverty and rife with insecurity. The thought of going back to that was now untenable. Yes, she had grown accustomed to a certain lifestyle. But she committed no crimes, suffered the verbal and physical assaults of a soulless man, was kind and generous to her family, and deserved to have love in her life. So, what a surprise blessing it was when she found it. And what an irony it was that Flemmi was the conduit for this unsuspecting romance. And what fun Debbie had dreaming about a life after Flemmi.

Those dreams may have begun in earnest as Detective Henault left that night with Flemmi. As Debbie closed the door, she was already thinking about the possibility of opening a new door—one that led to a castle where she could spend the rest of her life as a princess. A Mexican princess!

Debbie's new lover was a man named Gustavo. He was the handsome son of the poultry king of Mexico. He was heir to a fortune, the brother of a senator, and he just happened to be on the same cruise ship Debbie and Olga were on early in 1981. Gustavo first noticed Debbie's toned body as she laid out in the sun, and later he spotted her at lunch wearing a loose fitting sundress, and then again at dinner when she wore a skirt that was probably a little too tight for the occasion.

And each time Gustavo made his way around the ship to find Debbie, she had also noticed him. He was young, strong, olive-skinned, and he slicked his black hair until it shined like volcanic glass. Debbie watched Gustavo watching her. His was a stare, not quite a leer, but a long gaze that may have suggested love at first sight. For Debbie it was more like love at first blush. Gustavo had a direct way of letting his feelings known. It didn't take Debbie long to warm up to her new suitor.

Flemmi had paid for the mother-daughter getaway, and he'd pay for a few more vacation trips before realizing that he was facilitating the trysts between Debbie and Gustavo. As his suspicions rose, so did his anger. Once while Debbie was away in Acapulco, Flemmi searched Olga's house looking for incriminating evidence that Debbie was having an affair. Flemmi had plenty of women on the side, but he didn't like his women to have men on the side.

Poor Jay Antonelli found that out soon enough. A good Southie kid with a growing infatuation for Debbie, Antonelli had no idea that Flemmi had claimed exclusive rights to Debbie, even when they weren't a couple anymore. So, Antonelli was as surprised as he was petrified when Flemmi and Bulger grabbed him off the street one day and told him to stay away from Debbie. The threat worked.

Another courtship was cut short when a young admirer named Daniel Jassey was beaten to death in the Blue Hills of Canton. His murder has never been solved. And yet another guy Debbie had dated some time before turned up dead in the trunk of Ronnie's car. That was "Florida Paul," and his death was unrelated to any romantic jealousies. He was a counterfeiter who allegedly went to Suffolk Downs racetrack in East Boston to clean some money, and just coincidentally went to Eddie Davis's garage and bought Ronnie's Buick Riviera. When "Florida Paul" was found dead in the trunk, federal agents came to the garage looking for Ronnie because the car was still registered in his name.

"I sold him the car," Ronnie said producing a receipt to prove it. "But he never paid me in full," Ronnie lied. "So, I guess it's still my car. Do you know when I can get it back?"

That story always got a good laugh no matter how many times it was re-told. It was much funnier than the time Ronnie chased a friend down the street firing off gunshots until he found himself right in front of the Brookline Police Department. The humor was lost, because even though Ronnie was able to get away and ditch the gun, that incident led him to jail, and that was the beginning of the end.

Of all the Davis boys, Ronnie was the wildest. He drove through life at a hundred miles per hour, literally. He was riding at about that speed on his motorcycle when he was twenty-three years old. He sped past the family's Brookline garage, up School Street, and found himself at a construction site. A new school was being built, and Ronnie didn't see the giant hole he was racing toward. When the motorcycle crashed, the fiberglass gas tank split apart and gas spilled all over Ronnie. Then the motorcycle exploded.

Eighteen-year-old Steve Davis had seen Ronnie cruise by on the bike and then heard the explosion. He raced toward the sound and saw Ronnie, who was now a running ball of fire. Steve tackled him to the ground and was able to put the flames out, but not until Ronnie had suffered severe burns over 90 percent of his body.

Most people who knew him figured, given enough time, Ronnie would probably end up killing himself or someone else. He was a thief and a drug dealer, and much more of a wise guy than a tough guy.

Ronnie's downfall accelerated at a wedding thrown by Larry Baione and attended by Gennaro Angiulo, both leaders of the Boston Mafia. A lot of bad guys were at this joyful union and Ronnie pissed off all of them. "You ain't got no balls!" he shouted into the microphone. Ronnie was drunk and had pushed his way on to the stage. "You guys are punks! Not one of you guinea bastards has got any of these!" And this time he emphasized his point by grabbing his crotch. It was a genius move by anyone who wanted to get beaten beyond recognition. Ronnie was attacked by several of the guests and suffered multiple bruises, lacerations, and broken bones.

"When I saw him two days later," his brother Steve recalls, "he was still all swollen and black and blue."

Only one man at the wedding came to Ronnie's aid, and that was Nick Giso, a soldier in the Mafia. Giso was between a rock and a hard place. He was with Baione's crew, but he was also dating Ronnie's cousin, Liz McDonough. In order to keep a woman thirty years younger than himself, Giso had recently bought McDonough a new car. He paid for her apartment in Granada Highlands, and gave her $400 a week spending money. He also chose to obey her orders to "help Ronnie," which greatly upset his boss, Larry Baione.

Ronnie didn't think Giso did enough to help, so the first chance he had, he jumped Giso from behind, forced him down on his knees, and put a gun to his head. Tough guy Giso begged for his life and Ronnie let him go.

Soon after, Flemmi went to Ronnie and told him he was getting out of control, and that he would have to answer for it. Ronnie took the warning insouciantly and returned to his carefree lifestyle—until a few months later when the bars of the jail cell closed behind him. At the time of the wedding, Ronnie had been waiting to be sentenced for attempted breaking and entering in the daytime. Ronnie was sentenced to ten years and one day, which meant he'd do a year in Concord prison. But twenty-nine-year-old Ronnie Davis was abruptly transferred to Walpole prison and was dead in less than six months. Ronnie was still in Concord prison when guards did a random shake-down of his cell and found some pills. Ronnie swore the drugs were planted, and Steve Davis believes it was to ensure his transfer to Walpole where Flemmi had more control.

On St. Patrick's Day 1981, Ronnie was stabbed forty-seven times in the back. He was found near his cell at 9:30 p.m. during a routine check of the prisoners. It was a contract killing.

"The whole fucking thing was a set up," Steve Davis says. "Baione wanted Whitey to do something to settle this. But with Flemmi being my sister's boyfriend, no payback could happen. They wouldn't touch Ronnie without Flemmi's okay. Flemmi had to take care of it though. It had to be settled. Flemmi had connections in Walpole. He could make things happen. So, Ronnie was transferred from Concord to Walpole. Then he was stabbed."

Olga Davis was notified first of Ronnie's death. Shaken and distraught, she called her son, Steve, who went to Debbie's place in Brookline to tell her in person. Debbie was the sibling who visited Ronnie the most while he was locked up. Her visits were in defiance of Flemmi who didn't want her going to the prison. It was some ironic twist of chivalry that he didn't think a prison was the kind of place a girl like his Debbie should be seen. The two of them argued about it often, but Debbie made regular trips first to Concord and then to Walpole.

When Steve Davis got to Debbie's apartment, Flemmi was sitting on a couch reading a magazine. He glanced up as Debbie greeted her brother at the door, but he didn't seem too interested in the ensuing conversation. Perhaps he already knew.

"Ronnie just got murdered," Steve blurted. He waited a moment for that shocking news to register with Debbie. Then he added. "He got stabbed to death."

Debbie began screaming, and sobbing, and breathing heavily. Flemmi watched from his position on the couch. He didn't get up to console his girlfriend, nor did he ask any questions. He was remarkably calm, simply taking news of a murder in stride. When Debbie finally began to settle down, she still had no words for a while. Then she had an earful for Flemmi. "You better take care of this fucking thing!" she shouted. "You know people in Walpole. You better straighten this out. Find out who killed my brother!"

Flemmi nodded and said that he would. Then he returned to his magazine.

"Do it now!" Debbie screamed and Flemmi jumped. He gave Debbie a kiss on her head and left quickly. As the door closed behind him, Steve Davis began to say something, but his sister put her finger in the air signaling him to keep quiet. She listened for any type of movement in the hall. She waited for the sound of the elevator. She looked through the peephole and saw no one. So, after several minutes passed she opened the door, trying to do so nonchalantly in case someone— Flemmi—was out there. The coast was clear. "That cocksucker! That prick! He shouldn't have been home tonight," she said.

"What are you talking about?" Steve asked.

"They run card games every Tuesday night at the Marconi Club and a few other bars," Debbie explained. "He's always out on Tuesdays. But he was home tonight. Why? That prick was waiting for the call. He wanted to be here when I found out."

Again, just like with Eddie Davis, there was no hard evidence, but the Davis family sure found it coincidental that a few months after Flemmi said, "If he wasn't your father, he'd be a dead man," he was, in fact, a dead man. And soon after Flemmi told Ronnie he had something to answer for, Ronnie was killed by one or more people with whom he had no known problem.

The Davis's immediately suspected Flemmi and Bulger either ordered the hit on Ronnie as a favor to Angiulo and Baione, or they approved it. Their suspicion that it was, in fact, a contract killing was verified by a document found inside Bulger's FBI informant file. The document was filed on April 6, 1981, three weeks after Ronnie was killed. The Davis family would learn as of June 27, 2013, that:

> Source provided detailed information of a falling out in the Mafia between Larry Baione and Nick Giso over a murder in Walpole state prison in which the victim was the friend of Giso's girlfriend. Larry Baione ordered the "hit" due to an insult aimed at him by the victim in the past.

Information inside Flemmi's FBI informant file offered corroboration two weeks later:

> On 4/22/81 source advised that a kid named Anthony Malerva is the kid who took out Ron Davis in Walpole on orders from Larry "Baione" Zannino. Davis punched an individual at a wedding several months ago and Baione was very embarrassed. Larry reached out through the East Boston outfit people and got the word in to MCI-Walpole to "take out" Davis. Source speculated that Liz McDonough would have to know that Davis' death was no "accident" and is probably bitter towards Baione.

There continues to be questions about the accuracy of information found in Bulger and Flemmi's informant files, but their similar stories echo the truth in regards to the wedding, the fight, and the rift. Plus, Malerva was a Mafia wannabe with hopes of becoming a made man when he got out of prison. He never got the chance.

After Ronnie's blood was found on a T-shirt in Malerva's cell, Malerva was charged with Ronnie's murder. Not surprisingly, no witnesses stepped forward, and Malerva was found not guilty. The Davis family was livid. Steve, Mickey, and Victor let their anger be known, and talked a tough game on the streets. Upon Malerva's release from prison two years later, Flemmi called Steve Davis and told him to be careful, because Malerva wanted to get to the Davises before they got to him. Malerva was shot and killed on McLellan Highway in Revere. He was out of prison for three days.

"How did you hear that he was killed?" Olga was asked in a deposition years later.

"Someone called me up and told me."

"What was that person's name."

"I'm not going to reveal it. She just called and told me. She thought that I would want to hear it, that I would like to hear that he got killed."

"Did you like to hear it?"

"I didn't mind. He killed my son, didn't he?"

The woman who told Olga was Liz McDonough. She maintained her ties to the Mafia and claims Malerva was killed as part of Flemmi's elaborate cover-up. She believes Flemmi had Ronnie killed, in part, because Ronnie had once picked Flemmi's pocket while Flemmi was sleeping at Debbie's. Flemmi woke up feeling like a fool, and he never forgot it. When Flemmi saw an opportunity to have Ronnie killed and make it look like the Mafia did it, he pounced. Later, however, Flemmi had worries that Malerva would reveal the plan. This, again, from Bulger's FBI informant files:

> On 10/27/82 source advised that Nick Giso's girlfriend, Liz McDonough, told Phil Waggenheim that a kid named Malerva, who is supposed to be going on trial for the murder of Ron Davis in the "can," is now cooperating with the law and is saying that the "hit" on Davis was a "contract."

Malerba's murder was never solved, and there would be another attempted contract killing. The mobsters who pretended to live by some sort of code that included not killing women went after Liz McDonough. Four months after Ronnie's death, the following appeared in Bulger's informant file:

> On 7/10/81 . . . Source advised that Giso is concerned that the outfit people might be considering "taking out" Liz McDonough because of all of the problems she had had with Peter Limone, Joe Belliro, and Larry Baione. Larry blames McDonough for selling drugs to Larry's son, Joey Zannino.

The threat was corroborated when John Morris met Bulger and Flemmi at the Hotel Colonnade and played a tape from a wiretap for them in which the mob bosses talked openly about killing McDonough.

It took three years, but on March 20, 1984, a masked man shot McDonough three times in the head outside a dive bar called One If By Land on Commercial Street in Boston. Miraculously, McDonough survived. She told police she thought her attacker was a well-known drug dealer. But upon further reflection while serving eighteen years in prison for a series of robberies, McDonough came to believe Flemmi ordered the hit on her for two reasons, in particular. First, she challenged him on more than one occasion about Debbie's whereabouts. Second, she had once tried to kill Flemmi's daughter, Stephanie Hussey. "Oh, it was premeditated," Liz says without regret. "I didn't know who she was at the time." Liz says she was at a club called The Intermission in early 1981 when Stephanie called her the worst thing you can call a woman, so Liz left and waited outside in her car. When Stephanie came out, Liz hit the gas, and Stephanie hit her windshield. Stephanie was not badly hurt, and the criminal case against Liz was eventually dropped. "Whitey really came through for me," she says. "He got fifteen witnesses to say it wasn't me. But Stevie was so mad his nostrils were hitting his ears."

Flemmi accused Liz of putting herself in the middle of an ongoing war between Debbie Davis and Deborah Hussey. Those two hated each other and fought all the time, Liz says. So, Flemmi thought Liz went after one of the Hussey girls to please Liz's cousin, Debbie Davis. "That's why I got shot," Liz says with conviction. The mystery of who shot Liz McDonough has never been solved.

Meanwhile, Flemmi paid for Ronnie's funeral and tombstone, and went right on seeing Debbie. Despite her suspicions that he may have had something to do with her brother's death, and despite her increasing knowledge of Flemmi's criminal past and present, Debbie wasn't quite ready to make a clean break.

During the summer of 1981, Debbie made at least two trips to Brownsville, Texas, where she picked up a Ferrari and drove across the Mexican border to be with Gustavo, while she was also making plans to marry Flemmi. Imagine how Olga must have felt as she sat in her kitchen one day and listened to Debbie tell her how exciting it would be to move to Mexico to be with Gustavo, and on the very next day, hearing Flemmi say that he and Debbie were going to be married. "He was over my house, down in the living room," Olga said. "And he had his arms around Debbie and he says, 'We're getting married in September.'"

Flemmi went so far as to take a trip to Haiti ostensibly to finally get a divorce from Jeanette. For some reason he took Mickey Davis with him. Mickey thought the trip was some kind of drug deal, because Flemmi carried around a briefcase the whole time they were there, and never pursued any activity that would help him get a divorce.

When Flemmi was questioned under oath in the wrongful death suit filed by the Davis, Hussey, and Litif families in 2009, he claimed that his wife had wanted the divorce. And when he was asked about the nature of his relationship with Mickey Davis, he said, "I didn't have any relationship. I knew who he was. He was her [Debbie's] brother. Never socialized with him, and I never did any drugs with him." As for the divorce being the reason for the trip, Flemmi testified, "That might have been the reason. I never told him that."

And then there was the pregnancy. Debbie, who loved kids, and desperately wanted to have children some day, did the math and determined that there was no way the child was Gustavo's. It was Flemmi's. "I can't have this child," Debbie told her sister, Eileen. "It would be like bringing up the devil."

So, Eileen told Debbie to pack up and leave. Debbie could go to Mexico and live with Gustavo. He lived in a well-guarded mansion. Debbie would be safe there.

"I can't just pick up and go to Mexico," Debbie explained. "He [Flemmi] told me if I go to Mexico that my brothers and sisters would be killed one by one." Unlike Marion Hussey and Olga Davis, who both did their best to remain as ignorant as possible, Debbie Davis was too close to the situation not to know what she was up against. At night, she went to bed with a monster, and in the morning, she would wake up, try to wash the sins off with a hot shower, and then try to live as normal a life as possible. She took long walks with her mother, shopped with her sisters, partied with her friends, and dreamed.

Ten days after Ronnie's death, Debbie turned twenty-six. She was young and beautiful. She drove nice cars, wore nice clothes, and told herself she was happy. But in reality, she was scared. All day and every day, somewhere in the back of her mind was the incessant, nagging feeling that her whole life was only what it was because Flemmi allowed it. Her life—her very existence—was dependent upon the wishes and the whim of a monster she went to bed with at night.

"Just go," Eileen persisted. She was undeterred by the knowledge that Flemmi might kill her and her siblings. "Because after he kills one or two of us, they're going to find him. The Feds will know he did it, and they'll put him away."

In the end, Debbie decided not to escape to Mexico. She stayed with Flemmi, but she had an abortion. Debbie never told Flemmi she was pregnant, but somehow he found out she'd had the abortion. He may have been having her followed, because when she returned from the clinic, Flemmi was waiting to confront her. Debbie issued a series of half-hearted denials, first saying she wasn't at the clinic, then saying she had a miscarriage, before finally admitting to the abortion.

"You killed my baby!" Flemmi said with equal parts disappointment and genuine anger.

You killed my brother, Debbie may have thought, but remained silent.

That summer, Debbie returned to Mexico with her mother, and as they lay on the beach, Debbie said wistfully that she didn't want to go back to Boston. At that moment, running away seemed like a viable way out, but Olga told her the right thing to do was to look Flemmi in the eye, and tell him she was leaving him. It was the mature and socially gracious thing to do, but it was not without risk.

By then, Debbie already knew too much. Flemmi was constantly making abrupt departures from dinners and other engagements with Debbie, running off to meet with either Bulger or his "handler," a corrupt FBI agent named John Connolly. Each time, Debbie would either nag him about being Bulger's errand boy, or question him about why he had such a tight relationship with an FBI agent. When the excuses or his patience finally ran out, Flemmi told Debbie he and Bulger were working with the FBI. He wouldn't have admitted to being a top echelon informant, because despite providing the FBI with information in return for protection from criminal prosecution, Flemmi didn't consider himself an informant. U.S. Attorney Lawrence Eiser asked him, "Your understanding of your corrupt relationship with Connolly and the FBI was that you were authorized to engage in bookmaking and loan-sharking. Is that right?" Flemmi replied, "That's pretty much so. . . . That's why I considered it a quid pro quo. I didn't consider myself an informant."

The FBI, however, did consider him one of their best informants, which is why they included the initials "TE" (top echelon) on his informant card, which also included his informant number (137-2387), and listed him as the owner of Mount Pleasant Realty at 608 Dudley Street, Roxbury, Massachusetts. It was official. Flemmi worked for the FBI, and so did Bulger.

FBI agent Dennis Condon, a holdover from the Rico era, originally opened Bulger as an organized crime informant in 1971, but Bulger was closed due to lack of productivity.

Undeterred, Condon went to a casual meeting with Bulger, Flemmi, and Connolly at a coffee shop in Newton in 1974. It was clear the FBI, in its effort to bring down the Mafia, was attempting to forge another strong and symbiotic relationship with Bulger and Flemmi during that time.

Connolly re-opened Bugler as an informant in September 1975. Again, Bulger was closed, but then again re-opened on May 4, 1979. His informant file number was 137-4075, and his informant file card indicated he lived at 252 O'Callahan Way in South Boston, and that he worked for the Suffolk County Maintenance Department.

Connolly's special interest in Bulger began with his special relationship with Bulger's brother, Billy, the newly elected president of the Massachusetts senate. Connolly considered Billy to be his mentor. In an expression of gratitude, Connolly told Billy Bulger if there was anything he could ever do for him, all he had to do was ask.

"If you can keep my brother out of trouble, that would help," Billy replied.

Connolly obliged. He kept a close eye on Whitey. He met with him a few times a month, talked to him frequently on the phone, and they both had beepers so they could reach each other instantly. Bulger and Connolly were extremely close. Kevin Weeks, who saw Bulger nearly every day for thirteen years, thought that was because Bulger was paying Connolly for information, and that Connolly wanted to please Bulger. "John Connolly idolized Jim Bulger," Kevin Weeks testified later.

Flemmi would one day produce documents during a debriefing with the government leading to a plea agreement that would show he and Bulger gave Connolly approximately $235,000 between 1979 and 1990. The money came from what Flemmi and Bulger called the "EX Fund." It was a slush fund that they made deposits to with a percentage of each "score." In return, Connolly kept them out of jail.

"There's no way to look at your group giving John Connolly over $200,000 as anything other than a blatant act of corruption," Eiser asserted during the 2009 trial. "Isn't that right?"

"I would think so," Flemmi responded. "I mean, if he took the money, he's corrupt. He crossed the line."

However Flemmi described the relationship with Connolly, Debbie certainly had reason to believe he was an informant, and eventually Bulger found out about her suspicions. After Ronnie was killed in Walpole, Debbie told Flemmi to ask John Connolly to look into it. Both Connolly and Bulger were upset about that. Then as Flemmi and Debbie's relationship grew more and more strained, he was open to conversations with Bulger about getting rid of her.

"I said I wanted to send her away," Flemmi testified during Bulger's trial. "He said, 'You gotta kill her. You don't know what she said or to who.'" According to Flemmi, he initially argued that Debbie was no greater a risk than Bulger's girlfriends Cathy Greig and Theresa Stanley, who also knew about Connolly, or Connolly's wife, Maryann, who met Bulger on several social occasions. But Bulger eventually prevailed. "I eventually agreed," Flemmi testified. "And it happened. It's affected me, and it's going to affect me until the day I die."

There apparently was no rush to get rid of Debbie. Debbie's first indication that Flemmi may have been an informant came on her twenty-sixth birthday in March 1981. Ten days after Ronnie's death, Flemmi took Debbie out for her birthday. They went to the Bay Tower Room at the Prudential Center, but Flemmi had to leave early.

"Where are you going?" Debbie asked. "You can't leave me here alone on my birthday!"

"Jim wants to see me," Flemmi explained.

"It's another woman, isn't it?" Debbie accused. And the more she persisted in the allegation, the less convincing Flemmi's answers were, until he finally blurted out the truth. "We got a special connection. John Connolly. FBI agent," Flemmi stammered. "We have to go see him now."

Debbie stared at him for a moment. She was initially bewildered, but began to understand. Flemmi kissed her on the top of her head and took off. Dinner arrived a moment later, and Debbie dined alone on her birthday.

It remains Flemmi's contention, and his testimony, that he and Bulger talked "a few times" about killing Debbie, because she knew about their relationship with Connolly. He says he tapped Debbie's phone, which may be why he's so convinced that she told her brother, Mickey Davis, about Connolly. "She obviously said something to her brother," Flemmi testified. "And the fact that her brother became knowledgeable of that information, in Jim Bulger's eyes, was a serious offense. Jim Bulger is very sensitive about that." Flemmi asserts that Mickey was an informant, and that increased his concern and Bulger's about what Debbie might have told him, but the timeline suggests Flemmi is lying about this. Mickey didn't become an informant until he was picked up with a kilo of cocaine in his car in 1983. That was almost two years after Flemmi and Bulger had already killed Debbie. Furthermore, since Mickey was a drug dealer and user, and therefore not to be trusted, why not just kill him? The answer may be that Bulger had his reasons for wanting Debbie dead, and Flemmi had his own. He says he knew all about Gustavo, and admits to being a little jealous, but not enough to kill her over it. "She was a young girl," Flemmi says. "She wanted a family some day. I told her she could leave any time she wanted. If I was a jealous person, I wouldn't be sending her off to meet other people."

Yet, Debbie knew about Connolly for seven months before she was killed. Flemmi had only just learned about the seriousness of her relationship with Gustavo. When Debbie returned from her last trip to Mexico, she told Flemmi she was leaving him. She showed him her plane ticket for a return trip to Mexico. That information is in an FBI report filed by James Crawford on March 3, 2000. The report added that Debbie "was last seen at the Marconi Club which was controlled by the Winter Hill Gang, and she never made the flight for which she was registered."

On the last day of her life, Debbie appears to have been at her mother's house with her sister Eileen. Debbie did her mother's hair, and after dinner, the three women walked up to Randolph Center for ice cream, and strolled past some new homes being built. When they got back home, they sat in the kitchen for about twenty minutes when the phone rang. It was Flemmi. Olga gave the phone to Debbie who said, "What do you want?" and not much else. Then she said, "I have to go," to her mother and sister as she hung up. "He wants me to come home." Debbie kissed them both, said "I love you," and vowed to call her mother the next day. It was a promise she wouldn't keep.

Debbie stopped first at the Marconi Club, and called her mother from there. Olga was certain of this, because her friend, Paul, was the manager of the Club, and after she talked with Debbie, Paul got on the line for a few moments.

The last time Debbie Davis was seen alive by anyone other than Flemmi and Bulger, she was at the Marconi Club, yet no member of law enforcement ever interviewed anyone who was at the Club that night. An FBI agent would later testify that there was a dirt floor basement at the Club, and there was concern that Flemmi may have killed her and buried her there. No one checked the basement. No one questioned Flemmi. No one even interviewed Paul.

CHAPTER FOUR

Without a Trace

The story goes that after Flemmi's mother was mugged in Mattapan in 1979, Flemmi wanted to move her and his father into a better neighborhood. So, he bought them the house at 832 East Third Street in South Boston. Flemmi knew this to be a good neighborhood as Whitey Bulger's brother, Billy, lived next door, and Flemmi's good friend Pat Nee had a brother, Michael, who owned the house diagonally across at 799 East Third.

And it was a good, close-knit neighborhood in 1979, but in the next few years, four gruesome murders would take place there. Of course, this didn't dissuade Flemmi from thinking it was a safe place for his parents to live. After all, he participated in the murders. The most active murder location was at 799 East Third. That's where Bucky Barrett, John McIntyre, and Deborah Hussey were all killed and originally buried. Of those three, Barrett was first.

Arthur "Bucky" Barrett, made the mistake of failing to cut Bulger and Flemmi in on the Medford Bank Depository heist on

Memorial Day weekend in 1980. So, Flemmi and Bulger tried to extort money from him, but Barrett was a close associate of Frank Salemme. "So we backed off," Flemmi says. However, three years later Bulger and Weeks bumped into Barrett in the Prudential Center in Boston. That chance meeting put Barrett back on the radar for Flemmi and Bulger who then devised another plan to extort money from him. Bulger and Flemmi told Barrett they had some diamonds they wanted to fence, and they arranged a meeting at 799 East Third. Jimmy Martorano brought Barrett to the house. Kevin Weeks, Pat Nee, and John Martorano were already there as well. Bulger immediately put a gun to Barrett's head and ordered the others to chain him to a chair. The chains were merely an additional means to terrorize Barrett, who quickly divulged to his assailants that he had $60,000 in cash behind the washing machine at his home, and another $10,000 at Little Rascals, the bar he owned in Fanueil Hall. They had Barrett call his wife to make sure she wouldn't be home, and then Bulger and Flemmi went over and got the money. Weeks and Pat Nee stood guard while Barrett whispered a series of prayers.

After Flemmi and Bulger returned from Barrett's house, Weeks was given the assignment of retrieving the money at Little Rascals, and he chose to enlist the help of Barry Wong. It was a random choice. Wong was simply a guy who hung out at Triple O's and had become friendly with Weeks. Weeks picked up Wong and told him to go into Little Rascals where a man would hand him a brown paper bag. Wong was certainly aware of Weeks' reputation, so he went along and didn't ask any questions. Wong wasn't inside Little Rascals for more than a minute when he walked back outside and handed Weeks the bag. Weeks raced back to Michael Nee's house and gave the $10,000 to Bulger.

Bulger wanted more money, so Barrett put in a call to Joe Murray, Boston's largest marijuana dealer, and asked him for some cash. Barrett threatened to rat on Murray and everyone else he knew anything about. Murray hung up on him. Several hours had passed before Bulger announced that Bucky Barrett was going to "go downstairs and lay down for a while." They unchained Barrett and led him toward the basement.

Bulger pulled the trigger on his Mac-10 fully automatic machine gun, but nothing happened. He took his glasses off and noticed the safety was on. Bulger smiled a little at his silly mistake, switched the safety to off, and shot Barrett in the back of the head.

"I was right in front of him," Flemmi testified. "The bullet could've gone through him and hit me. The body did hit me and we both fell down the stairs."

However, the version of the Barrett murder story memorialized in a written report by Massachusetts State Police Lieutenant Steve Johnson indicates that Flemmi said he was actually in the kitchen when Bulger pulled the trigger.

Once in the basement, Flemmi pulled out Barrett's teeth with the dental pliers they had gotten from Bulger's girlfriend, Cathy Greig, who was a dental hygienist. Bulger went upstairs to lie down while Flemmi and Weeks dug a hole and buried Barrett beneath the basement's dirt floor. When asked why they buried him in the basement, Flemmi said, "It was a convenient location for one thing."

It was another ruse that brought McIntyre to 799 East Third Street on November 30, 1984. He'd been told he could buy into a drug deal for $20,000 in cash. Instead, when he got to the house, Bulger stepped out from behind a refrigerator and shoved a submachine gun into his chest. When McIntyre stumbled backward, Weeks caught him and wrestled him to the floor. Like Barrett he was shackled to a chair at gunpoint. Bulger interrogated him about two crimes in particular that

McIntyre was involved in. One was a marijuana shipment that had been intercepted by the DEA. The other was a weapons shipment that had gone bad. In that second case, seven tons of weapons had been shipped from Gloucester, Massachusetts, on the *Valhalla* to the IRA in Ireland. Some of the weapons on board were provided by Bulger and Flemmi.

The cargo was off-loaded on to the *Marita Ann*, which was subsequently seized by Irish authorities off the coast of Ireland. When the load was seized, the assumption was that someone had tipped off the authorities. Bulger already knew that when the *Valhalla* returned to Boston, McIntyre was on board, but hadn't been arrested. The only possible explanation was that McIntyre had talked to U.S. Customs. And according to Weeks, FBI agent Connolly confirmed this. Now, Bulger wanted McIntyre to admit it.

McIntyre quickly confessed, but remained shackled for nearly six hours while his future was discussed over dinner. At some point in the afternoon, Bulger decided to kill McIntyre and Flemmi concurred. Bulger grabbed a boat rope, tied it around McIntyre's neck and began strangling him. But the rope was too thick, and McIntyre merely gurgled and started vomiting. "This ain't working. You want one in the head?" Bulger asked his victim.

McIntyre begged, "Yes, please," and Bulger shot him. Flemmi then grabbed McIntyre by his hair and held him up, while Bulger shot him a few more times.

"He's dead now," Bulger announced.

They split up the $20,000 Customs had given to McIntyre for the presumed drug deal, and McIntyre's body, stripped and toothless, was buried in the basement.

Sometime early in 1985, Deborah Hussey was also lured to 799 East Third Street. Flemmi has testified on several occasions

body of Debbie Davis would be dumped in the same general location.

What happened during the final moments of Debbie Davis's life will forever remain a mystery, unless you believe the accounts of Kevin Weeks, who wasn't there, and Steve Flemmi, who was far from the pillar of truthfulness. With a wife, a common law wife, a mistress, and sordid affairs with teenagers, Flemmi's entire life was a lie. He lied to the women in his life and the men he did business with, sometimes right up until the moment he killed them.

And yet, his is the only story we have as to what happened to Debbie Davis on September 17, 1981. He says he took Debbie to breakfast that morning, and they made plans to meet later at the house he had just bought for his parents at 832 East Third Street. Flemmi would leave the breakfast to sign papers that would finalize the purchase. He was buying the home from a friend of Whitey Bulger's and was given access to the house and permission to begin renovations even before the deal was official. For that reason, the house was empty except for the tools and tarps left by the contractors at the end of their work day. Flemmi told Debbie they would go to the house to inspect the work being done. Unbeknownst to Debbie, Bulger was already there.

The door to the house was unlocked. Flemmi turned the knob and walked in ahead of Debbie. The living room would have been on her left. Unsuspectingly she continued to follow Flemmi down the hallway passing the kitchen and a large dining area. It was a narrow corridor, and it was dark. Did she feel a bit of uneasiness as she passed the first bedroom?

Flemmi and Bulger had hatched this plan to lure Debbie to the house, and to her certain death, but the details were vague. Flemmi didn't know exactly how this would go down.

He didn't know Bulger was hiding in that first bedroom. Silent and blood-thirsty, Bulger pounced. He grabbed Debbie from behind, scissored her neck between his forearms and began to crush her windpipe.

Debbie fought for her life. She was strong, and she was tough. Whitey Bulger was grappling with a woman who once put the point of her spiked high heel shoe through another girl's cheek. Debbie wore fine clothes and dined in nice restaurants now, but she was from the streets. She was the same woman who unrepentantly slammed her brother, Steve, in the face with a bicycle handlebar. Bulger was in for a fight.

Bulger pulled Debbie toward the basement. She kicked and pushed and thrashed about, but Bulger never relinquished his grip on her. He finally had his hands around the woman who had smart-mouthed and disrespected him so many times through the years. He put up with it because she was Flemmi's girl, but it always upset him.

Unable to breathe, Debbie's heart raced. Finally, the realization that she was about to die must have hit her. She looked up and saw Flemmi, the man whom she had been with for nearly ten years, who had lavished her with luxuries, and who had often told her he loved her.

He stood by and watched as she breathed her last breath. "Let her pray!" Flemmi cried out, but it was too late.

Debbie never got the chance to say one last prayer. She never had a chance to say good-bye to her family, or to raise one of her own. She never had the chance to really experience love, or simply to experience her twenty-seventh birthday. With Bulger's arms wrapped around her throat for the final two or three minutes of her life, Debbie Davis never had a chance. Despite the life she chose and the company she kept, she deserved a better fate than this.

The basement door was already open. Bulger, in his inimitable way, had prepared the scene before Flemmi and Debbie arrived. He had the lights out and the curtains drawn. While he waited, he peered out the window at the house next door. That was the home of his brother, Billy, already the president of the Massachusetts State Senate. The houses were right on top of one another, and only a few feet separated where Whitey stood from Billy's kitchen. And he knew there was always the possibility that Billy could walk into Flemmi's parents' home at any time, because Billy, who didn't allow a television in his own home, regularly walked unannounced into the Flemmi household to watch TV. Whitey either knew Billy wasn't home, or he was aroused by the uncertainty. Either way, he was about to squeeze the life out of an innocent woman and then bring her body down to the basement. So, he needed the basement door open. Everything needed to be just so.

Bulger and Flemmi carried Debbie's body to the basement, dropping it once along the way. Flemmi claims Bulger helped him remove Debbie's clothing and wrap her body in the tarp, and then went back upstairs and laid down. "There was no furniture, and he just laid down on a rug on the floor," Flemmi testified.

Flemmi began to rip Debbie's teeth out with pliers so that it would be harder to identify the body if it were ever found, but he maintains he was too emotionally distraught to extract all the teeth, only mustering up the strength to rip out a couple of them. "I couldn't do it," he testified, indicating the same emotional response that he had to Deborah Hussey's murder. "I couldn't go through with it." But he did go through with the plan to murder her. And Weeks, who wasn't there, says Flemmi knelt down and whispered in his dead girlfriend's ear, "You're going to a better a place."

Perhaps, her spirit was, but her body was tossed into the trunk of a car and brought to a garage in Quincy. Flemmi testified that Bulger enlisted the help of Jack Curran and Pat Nee, and all four of them waited until later in the evening to covertly dispose of the body in a marshy area beneath the Neponset River Bridge.

"We dug the hole while she was there," Flemmi testified as Bulger sat silently at his trial. "We carried the body about ninety yards. I dug the hole. We buried the body." Flemmi stated that Bulger sat on the river bank and watched him dig the hole and push the body into the grave.

"Why isn't Jim Bulger doing any of the work?" Flemmi was asked.

"That's what he does," Flemmi responded.

Flemmi didn't sleep much that night. By 5:00 a.m. he was back at Olga's house rousting Eileen out of bed. He barged right into her bedroom and pulled the sheets off her. He appeared to be an emotional wreck. He was both angry and distraught, ranting and raving that Debbie had left him. Flemmi ordered Eileen to get up and go with him to Debbie's place to look for any clues about where she had gone. Confused, but curious, Eileen obeyed. She was still in her pajamas as she looked through Debbie's things.

Flemmi focused on the possibility that Debbie had gone to Mexico, but Eileen couldn't find any evidence of that. As far as she could tell, all of Debbie's clothes were still in the closet. Plus, if Debbie were going to leave, wouldn't she have told her sister, or her mother? At this point, Eileen couldn't even understand why Flemmi was so convinced that Debbie had left him. Just yesterday, Debbie had been at Olga's house doing her mother's hair, taking a relaxing walk, eating ice cream. In fact, the last thing she said was that she was leaving to meet

Flemmi. Maybe she was in an accident. Maybe she was with someone else, another man, or at a friend's house. It was odd to see Flemmi so convinced so early that Debbie had vanished with no real evidence supporting it. Finally, he calmed down and said, "Hey, let's go into the bedroom and have a little fun."

"You motherfucker!" Eileen shouted. "You tell me my sister is missing, and now you put the moves on me? You sick bastard!" If Eileen Davis had had any doubts about how evil, depraved, and damnable Flemmi was, those doubts were removed in that instant. If she had had any doubts that Debbie truly had disappeared, those doubts were erased later that day. Debbie didn't come home. She didn't call. And when Olga called her beeper, Flemmi responded. In fact, Flemmi kept that beeper until 1990.

Flemmi explained to Olga that Debbie told him she was going out to run errands. She took his car to the post office and then to the cleaners. He said the last time he saw her was the day before at the Marconi Club. He sat in Olga's kitchen and cried. More than once, tears rolled down his cheeks as he confided to Olga his love for Debbie and his sorrow that she may have left him for another man. He even told Olga that he and Bulger had gone to Mexico looking to hurt Gustavo, but they couldn't get near him.

"He's leading me to believe that she might be down there," Olga testified years later. "So it would take the heat off of me to think maybe I thought it was him that killed her. Gustavo's house was so well guarded, he couldn't have gone near it or he would have got the bullet. And it's too bad he didn't take two more steps and get that bullet."

Olga and Eileen went together to the Randolph police station two days after Debbie went missing to file a missing persons report. They brought photos of Debbie. They told the police where she lived, the places she frequented, and who some of her friends were, but they omitted a few pertinent details about Debbie's mobster boyfriend, even though Flemmi had told her it was fine with him if she told the police about his relationship with Debbie. "I wasn't sure if I should tell the police that Flemmi was Debbie's boyfriend because he was married, and he had a girlfriend and a bunch of kids," Olga would later claim. When U.S. Attorney Lawrence Eiser asked her in court whether she had told police that the last time she had seen her daughter, Debbie was planning to meet Flemmi, or that Flemmi answered Debbie's beeper, Olga said no.

It's hard to imagine what the Davis family went through in the days and weeks, and eventually years, that passed since the last time they saw Debbie. She had dated a violent criminal, and suddenly she was gone. "I tried to put two and two together," Olga would state in a deposition years later, "which added to four, okay?" But the math was fuzzy, the facts were ambiguous, and Flemmi was beguiling. For seven consecutive days after he aided in the murder of Debbie Davis, he went to her mother's house and wept. And he lied.

The picture he painted for Olga was of a lovelorn Romeo (himself) racing through Logan Airport frantically searching for his Juliet. He told her that he went to every airline and showed a picture of Debbie to dozens of ticket takers, baggage handlers, restaurant employees, and janitors, who all said they hadn't seen her.

He'd held Olga's hand and fought back the tears. He told Olga that a woman finally said that Debra had gotten on a plane, but as "Lisa" rather than Debra. According to Flemmi's story, Debbie was traveling under an alias for no apparent reason. The idea that she might have boarded a plane for Mexico was plausible. It even made sense. But why leave without saying a word to anyone? Why travel incognito? And why didn't she call when she reached her destination? Flemmi may have been an expert liar and master manipulator, but even he didn't have answers for those questions. "I just miss her," he said sadly. "I wish she would come back. I don't know why she left."

Olga and Eileen went again to the Randolph police station with more pictures of Debbie and her birth certificate. This time Olga told them that Flemmi was Debbie's boyfriend, but once again she didn't confide that Flemmi was the last person she was known to be with. While that would appear to be a glaring omission, the police still should have questioned Flemmi. They didn't. Even though Olga spoke with Randolph police on September 19, the National Crime Information Center didn't report Debbie as missing until nearly three weeks later on October 8, 1981. The request to search for her was canceled on March 29, 1982, when police received a tip that Debbie had been spotted, not in Mexico, but in Houston, Texas.

As the story became more and more convoluted, the Davises didn't know what to believe. Olga fell into a deep depression, barely mustering up enough energy to get out of bed in the morning. Thoughts raced through her mind—Debbie as a child, Debbie as a beautiful woman, Flemmi as a friend, Flemmi as a suspect. Canada. Mexico. Texas. Why couldn't the police find her daughter?

Olga had several meetings with FBI agents, and she couldn't help but notice how strange the meeting places were. She was told to drive behind a supermarket in Randolph where agents would be waiting in a dark colored car. There was a similar meeting behind a restaurant, and another one inside a small room at a Walpole motel. But as odd as the rendezvous locations were, the questions they asked Olga were even more unexpected: "What can you tell us about Whitey Bulger and Steve Flemmi's illegal activities?" "Have you ever seen Steve Flemmi with known criminals, or with law enforcement officials?" "Did your daughter ever tell you what she knew about Steve Flemmi or Whitey Bulger or their associates?"

At each meeting with the FBI, there would only be a few perfunctory comments updating the search for Debbie, and then a long series of probing questions about Bulger and Flemmi. The FBI seemed less interested in Debbie's whereabouts, and more interested in what she knew, and what she may have told about her boyfriend and his criminal counterpart.

"Every time I meet you," Olga finally said to one of the agents, "you talk about Steve and Whitey and not about my daughter."

"We gotta know about these guys," the agent responded. "They're dangerous. And don't forget you have eight other children."

That was the last time Olga Davis ever spoke to the FBI. She took the unnecessary reminder that she had eight other children as a threat. The agent couched his remark with concern for the safety of her kids, but the inference Olga drew from it was that if she said the wrong thing to the FBI, if they began to think she knew too much about Flemmi and Bulger, that her children could be in danger.

"If that ain't a fucking threat, what is?" Debbie's brother, Steve, wonders to this day. "They know everything about you. It's the government. When my mother went to get Debbie's pictures from the Randolph police, they were missing. Gone. And nobody's saying nothing. How deep does the conspiracy go? Everybody's protecting everybody. The government did my mother wrong."

Flemmi continued to visit Olga three or four times a week for several months after Debbie went missing. He swore to her that he was doing everything he could to find her. Olga found herself in the ironic position of consoling her killer. One night, Debbie's sister, Sandra, couldn't take it anymore. When she saw Flemmi blubbering like a baby in the kitchen and Olga and Eileen comforting him, she screamed, "You're the devil! You fucking killed my sister, and you know it. You fucking devil! And these two are too stupid to know it. They won't open their eyes." She slammed the door as she left the house. Eileen recalled getting goosebumps at her sister's accusation. Flemmi pretended to be insulted, but didn't bother to deny anything. When he left a few minutes later, Olga and Eileen must have worried whether he was off to find Sandra. It wasn't the first time Sandra had voiced her suspicions. It was just the first time she voiced them directly to Flemmi. But she was constantly scolding Michelle for spending too much time with Flemmi.

"You're just upset, because I don't want to be with *you*," Flemmi said to her one day.

Sandra was killed by a hit and run driver in 1993.

At Eileen's deposition years later, U.S. Attorney Eiser read from an AP news story from October 9, 2000, that stated, "Federal investigators arrived within two days and talked to her [Debbie's] mother who told them she believed the person responsible was Flemmi." He then asked her, "Do you remember your mother making that comment?" Eileen answered, "No, she never said that in two days. Would my mother let him back in the house if she thought he killed her? I don't think so."

By early November, about six weeks after Debbie's disappearance, Steve Davis asked Flemmi what he was going to do with Debbie's car and her apartment. Informed that there were no immediate plans, Steve gave Flemmi $15,000 for Debbie's Mercedes and then moved into her apartment.

"Where's that gonna put your head?" Steve thinks now. "He sold me everything she owned. If she comes back in the picture, what the fuck is she going to say? That cocksucker should have just gave it to me. Here, take it. And when she comes back, you can give it to her. He was still pretending to pine for her, yet he sold me everything. When that came about, I knew. I was just looking for clues."

There were certainly no clues at Debbie's apartment. Everything had been emptied out by the time Steve Davis moved in. It was a clear sign that Flemmi knew for a fact that Debbie wouldn't be returning. All her clothes, shoes, photos, personal items, and furniture were gone. Olga did have a key to a safety deposit box in Debbie's name which Debbie had given to her in case anything ever happened. Inside were three expensive pieces of jewelry.

Undoubtedly, they were gifts from Flemmi. What seemed like generosity would eventually be revealed as Flemmi's own insatiable greed. He gave gifts to women to feed his own avarice. He wanted what he couldn't otherwise have. So, he gave and he took. He gave Debbie the life she had always wanted. And then he took it away. Her body now lies next to her brother, Ronnie's, in a Randolph cemetery. A large tombstone, bought and paid for by Stephen Flemmi, marks Ronnie's final resting place. But there is no name on Debbie's stone. Steve Davis refuses to put her name on a stone that Flemmi bought.

CHAPTER FIVE

Missed Opportunity

People age quickly when a loved one is missing. Olga Davis wore the worry on her face every day. Debbie's brothers and sisters felt the sorrow and confusion eating them up inside. Debbie Davis simply vanished. She was there one day and gone the next without an explanation, or a good-bye, or a death to mourn. Where once there was a woman known for her kindness and lively spirit there was now just a void. A mysterious void.

"I knew she was dead after the first week," Steve Davis says. "I didn't think Flemmi so much. Maybe he would have been behind it, but not right in the middle of it, because I thought he loved her." He also thought Flemmi was his friend. There was a lot going through Steve Davis's mind in the days, months, and years following Debbie's disappearance. At times, he was convinced she was dead. Other times, he thought she might be in Canada or Mexico. He thought the police were trying to find her. He thought the FBI had threatened his mother.

He thought Debbie would never leave without saying a word. And he thought he might get a postcard from her some day explaining why she left. He thought a lot of things, but what he thought about more than anything was killing Flemmi.

"I fight in my head all the time with that," Steve Davis says now. "What could I have done? What should I have done? I don't want to sound like a coward, because I have no problem with doing the time. You got to adapt. Things didn't work out the way I wanted them to. So, today, I get real fucking angry. I mean angry. I don't know if I'm a fucking time bomb waiting to go off."

And that bomb has been ticking incessantly since the early hours after Debbie disappeared—with Steve's frustration of not knowing what happened, and his suspicion that Flemmi was involved. For Davis, the anger builds as the days pass and there are still no answers.

So, Davis lives every day with the regret of not killing his sister's killers. He spends little or no time anguished by the things he did, like being a drug dealer, becoming a heavy drug user, or finally being sent to jail after a multitude of robberies. Instead, he is haunted by what he didn't do, and what he believes in his heart he would have been justified in doing.

It was a missed opportunity to kill Whitey Bulger when he was summoned to Triple O's, and it was an unfortunate twist of fate that left Steve Davis standing alone in the woods outside his mother's house one night wearing a ski mask and watching Flemmi drive away.

Almost two years after Debbie was murdered, Flemmi was still spending time with Olga at her house in Randolph. He had even bought her a car. "It wasn't a new one," Olga would say, "but it was well kept." Meanwhile, Flemmi was also abusing Debbie's sister, Michelle.

Steve Davis didn't know about the abuse, but he hated that Flemmi was still hanging around. Olga knew this. So, one day when Steve called his mom on the phone, and she was unusually furtive, he sensed something was wrong.

"Is he there?" he asked.

Olga watched Flemmi sipping a cup of coffee at her kitchen table, and responded with a simple, "Yes."

Steve, as was his habit, paused before he lied. He told his mother he was heading down to Cape Cod for the day. Then he got his gun and a ski mask, hustled to his car, and drove quickly toward his mother's house. His heart pounded and his knees shook, and for the entire ride, he kept telling himself it was time to do this. "I was gonna kill him right in front of my mother."

He parked at the far end of Burris Way in Randolph and walked up the hill. He ducked in the woods and made his way without being seen. When he came to a spot where he could see Flemmi's Chevy Capris parked outside Olga's house, he pulled the ski mask over his face and pulled out his gun.

Suddenly, he noticed another car parked on Hollis Street, which intersected with Burris Way. It was hard to tell, but it looked like an Aries K-car, and someone was in the driver's seat with a clear view of Olga's house. That's odd, Davis thought. And so he backed up behind a tree and waited. In the several minutes that passed, Davis convinced himself that whoever was in that car was watching his mother's house. Cops? Maybe they were following Flemmi. Maybe they were there to track one of the drug dealing Davis boys.

Several more minutes passed, and Davis didn't make a move. His gaze went back and forth from the house to the car. His knees had long since stopped shaking. Whether it was fear or trepidation that made his heart race, that feeling was gone. He was immersed in the mystery of that car—wondering why it was there and hoping it would move so he could do what he had come to do.

Finally, Davis watched crestfallen as Flemmi walked out of the house and got into his car and simply drove away. Flemmi drove toward Hollis Street, looked to his right where the Aries K was parked, and turned left. The K-car followed him out of the neighborhood. Davis's paranoia was vindicated. He was right about that car, and right not to make a move on Flemmi. But he knew that it's a rare moment when a man has both the opportunity and courage to kill another man, and Davis never had that combination again. That was his best and last real chance to kill Flemmi, and it slipped away.

Instead, Davis went into his mother's house and asked her, as he so often did, if Flemmi had any new leads on where Debbie might be. The answer was always the same. Flemmi was no help. The police weren't trying very hard. And the Davis family's own investigation had only one lead—Gustavo. And as soon as Olga contacted him in Mexico and discovered Debbie wasn't there, the trail went cold. Of course, Gustavo could have been lying. If Debbie had run off to escape Flemmi, she would have instructed Gustavo to keep her secret. It might have been worth a trip to Mexico to see for themselves, but none of the Davis's ever took that initiative. In fact, other than Olga's infrequent visits with the FBI and Randolph police, there was no other contact between the family and investigators. "I wouldn't go to the law," Steve Davis says, admitting that his drug dealing and robberies made him reluctant to talk with the police about anything. "What I was doing then, I was waiting. I was cautious about what I was doing. I was waiting to be questioned along with everybody in the family. I didn't want my criminal activities getting tied up in all that."

But no one—repeat no one—in the family was questioned. It was bad enough that Flemmi was never questioned.

After all, he was the last person Debbie was known to have been with, and his reputation was less than stellar. But what about some routine questioning of Debbie's family members? Police might have asked where she liked to hang out, who some of her friends and associates were, if she had any enemies, whether she was involved with any shady characters. But Debbie Davis vanished without a trace and there was very little effort made to find out what happened. Flemmi's bogus story that Debbie was spotted in Texas gave investigators a reason to stop looking.

The Davis family talked and fretted and vented with each other, but while some may criticize their lack of real action—they didn't post flyers with Debbie's picture around the area, or make public complaints to the news media about an ineffective investigation, or hire a private investigator—it doesn't appear that any of this would have made a difference. There was no body. And nobody talking. Flemmi, Bulger, and eventually Weeks were the only ones who knew what happened. What could the Davis family do?

When Steve Davis decided to get married a police officer warned him that it might be a good time to get out of the drug business. Davis handed off all his customers to other dealers and went clean. "Like that Kenny Rogers song, 'You gotta know when to hold 'em and when to fold 'em. I've always had a good sense of that," Davis said. "And I knew it was time. I wanted to quit. I wanted to get married and start having kids. American dream."

The dream started with Susan Culhane. He'd been dating her for nearly ten years, but they were broken up in the summer of 1982. Despite that Davis took her out to a fancy Italian restaurant named Franco's in Norwood to discuss their future. Some time between the antipasto and the lasagna, Davis asked Susan to marry him.

"We'll get married when you have ten thousand dollars," she said.

Davis, who had $150,000 in cash wrapped in rolls of aluminum foil and taped to the bottom of a dresser drawer in Susan's apartment, just laughed. "I had my shoes custom made and shipped up from Florida," Steve brags. "Purple snakeskin boots. I was wearing an 8.5 carat diamond ring on my pinkie at the time. Unbelievable!"

It is truly amazing to think that after a decade of dating, Susan had no idea what Davis did or what he was worth. She drove the Cadillac d'Elegance he'd bought her. Davis had one, too. He also had the red Camaro and Debbie's old Mercedes he'd bought from Flemmi.

"Ten grand? Fuck you!" Davis said as the wedding proposal spiraled out of control. "Let's go. Get your shit."

On their way out of the restaurant, Davis was immediately sidetracked by Maryann Savini, a long-time family friend and a tall, beautiful blonde who lived in a building adjacent to Debbie Davis's old apartment where Steve Davis was now living. After a brief courtship, they were married first by a justice of the peace on October 20, 1982, and again during a more traditional ceremony one month later on November 27.

After the wedding, guests went to the Hyatt Regency for the first reception ever held in the Spinnaker Lounge, a room known for its rotating floor and panoramic views of Boston. As the wedding party emerged from the fleet of limos, Davis handed each passenger a vile of cocaine.

On the guest list were Adolph "Jazz" Maffie, who was part of the Great Brink's Robbery in 1950, and George Kaufman, who once ran Marshall Motors as a front for Howie Winter, and eventually did the same for Bulger and Flemmi at the Lancaster Street Garage. Kaufman had been a long-time friend of Steve

Davis's father, who was invited to the wedding by Olga, who also invited Flemmi with Steve's permission.

Steve Davis's suspicions that Flemmi had killed Debbie were still fairly strong at the time of the wedding, but he says, "If I didn't invite him, I'd be showing my hand." Davis and Flemmi had one conversation during the reception. It was initiated when Flemmi began telling people that Davis was paying for everybody's parking, which he wasn't. During the disagreement that followed, Flemmi made it clear that he believed it was customary for the host to cover the guests' parking fees. Davis told him to keep his nose out of it. "Why would I cover the parking? Let them pay for their own parking. I don't care where they park. I ain't paying for it."

Maryann and Steve Davis had a son, Steven, in 1983, a daughter, Janessa, in 1985, and a second daughter, Debbie, in 1988. Davis's sister Debbie by then had been missing for seven years and was presumed dead.

Davis had tried to go straight but landed in jail before Debbie's first birthday. He and his brother, Mickey, had purchased an empty lot in Hyde Park for $40,000. They got a license and permit to store up to 125 cars. They started with four rental cars and called the place "Dynasty Motors," named after the popular TV show, *Dynasty*.

Steve ran the business with Mickey, a silent, albeit, troublesome partner. In less than a month, Steve had twenty rental cars and business was booming. He was excited to be building something from the ground up, excited that even with just a sixth grade education, he could make big money as a legitimate businessman. But it was soon over.

In addition to his rental business, Steve had been selling three or four cars a week to a Boston police officer who fixed them up at his house and sold them on the side. One day the cop arrived with some alarming news. "They're gonna be raiding you, Steve." The cops knew what Steve didn't—that Mickey was selling large amounts of Percodan out of the garage at Dynasty Motors. So, after Steve caught Mickey red-handed with piles and piles of pills, he sold the business for $125,000 and gave Mickey his initial $20,000 investment. Mickey, of course, wanted an even split of the full sale price, but Steve told him to "go fuck himself."

Steve tried again, this time buying a gas station with a little variety store where he put his mother to work. It was there that Steve and Olga saw a newspaper ad for a department store. Olga started screaming and crying when she saw the beautiful model in the ad stretched out on the floor holding herself up on one elbow.

"It was a perfect double of my sister Debbie," Steve recalls. "The spitting image. And I thought she probably is off modeling somewhere."

Olga called the police and brought them the photo, but it didn't take long to find out the model was someone else. The Davises were reminded once again that hope is a dangerous thing, in part, because it's so closely connected to hopelessness. Steve Davis, who maintains he never did drugs when he was selling them, began dabbling with coke, taking some pills, and even started snorting heroin. He now considers it a weakness to blame his drug use on any level of sorrow, loneliness, or guilt regarding his sister's disappearance, but at the time he felt, "My head was so fucked up with this whole thing. Walking around trying to be quiet about something that can affect your whole family. I'm married with kids. I can't be so loud about it."

Davis didn't want to take money from the family budget to pay for his drug habit, so he started robbing houses again.

He had done it successfully for years when he was a kid. His last robbery, which included two accomplices, occurred at a home in Wellesley in 1989, for which he was sentenced to three to five years in prison. He served twenty-seven months in Walpole, Concord, and Bridgewater prisons. He was offered a chance to reduce the sentence if he gave up the name of the other man who was with him.

"Stand your ground," Maryann told him. "We'll be here when you get out." And they were. Maryann and the kids never visited Davis in prison, because he wouldn't allow them to, but Maryann stood by her man. She waitressed while Davis served his time.

"You get up in the morning," Steve Davis recalls his days in prison. "You play cards. By early afternoon, you're outside playing handball. You get a job in the kitchen. You eat good food. It's not great, but it's not something a guy should rat on another man for. I don't think a guy should give up his fucking oath, his loyalty, his honor to rat on somebody. It's not that bad. Hey, it gives you time to think about what you did wrong."

While he was incarcerated, Davis thought a lot about his sister, Debbie. Believing she must be dead, and that it was no accident, Davis assumed she'd been murdered and her body was buried somewhere. He became aware that dental records could be used to identify a body. So, he decided to take a job at the office of the Davis's family dentist. Once there, he'd steal Debbie's dental records and have them in case her body was ever discovered. But apparently, Flemmi had beat him to it.

George Kaufman's wife, Ruth, was the dentist's receptionist. When Davis found his entire family's dental records, except for Debbie's, he surmised that Ruth had taken them, given them to George, who then gave them to Flemmi, who must have destroyed them.

Davis's second trip to prison was due to a botched robbery at a Lechemere department store. A new partner of his went in to steal computers while Davis waited outside. He was waiting too long. Police arrived, and Davis was arrested for larceny. He was sent away for most of 1994 and part of 1995.

The best part of 1995 for Davis was when he learned that Flemmi had been arrested on federal extortion charges and handcuffed like a common criminal at Schooner's Restaurant on High Street in Boston. Flemmi had actually been tipped off that his arrest was imminent, but he mistakenly thought he had more time. "I procrastinated a few days," he testified flatly. The day I was leaving was the day I got arrested."

Police were also looking for Frank Salemme and Whitey Bulger. They found Salemme seven months later in West Palm Beach, Florida. There was no sign of Whitey Bulger. "There's no doubt we'll get Whitey," State Police Sgt. Thomas Foley told the *Boston Globe.* "It's just a matter of time." It took sixteen years.

The police should have been on the beach at the L Street Bathhouse in July 1995. There they would have seen Bulger appear like a ghost before the man perhaps most responsible for putting him on the run—Steven Rakes. When Rakes saw Bulger, he was so frightened, he ran to the ocean's edge, dove in, and started swimming. As he swam out into deeper waters of the Atlantic, he thought about how unfortunate he was to have had his life intersect with Whitey Bulger's and Steve Flemmi's.

About twelve years earlier, Rakes and his wife, Julia, had bought the South Boston Liquor Mart. They were a nice young couple ready to take a risk on a new business and see where hard work might take them. Instead, they found themselves on the wrong end of Bulger's wrath and a loaded gun.

Rakes' sister, Mary O'Malley, was a drug dealer under the Winter Hill umbrella, and according to Kevin Weeks, she went to him and said the Rakes wanted to sell. That seems unlikely since the Rakes had only owned the liquor store for a few weeks. Regardless, Bulger, Flemmi, and Weeks told Steven Rakes they were going to buy the store from him. They brought $67,000 in cash to his home on Ford Street and expected to finalize the deal. As Bulger sat with the Rakes's one-year-old daughter, Megan, on his lap, Rakes said he didn't want to sell the store. Weeks thought Rakes was trying to get more money out of them, so he took out his gun and placed it on the table for Rakes to see.

"The girl reached for the gun," Weeks said. "Jim Bulger pushed it back to me and said, 'Put it away.' Then he says to Rakes, 'We had a deal. You ain't backing out!'"

Rakes agreed to sell the store. Julia Rakes was livid. She got in touch with her uncle, Joseph Lundbohm, a Boston police detective, and told him what had happened. Lundbohm made the mistake of contacting John Connolly, who immediately told Bulger about the complaint against him. Undeterred, Bulger went back to the Rakes and told them they'd better back off. This time they did and they sold him the store. The Rakes then went on a family vacation to Disney World in Florida. Since Rakes wasn't around, there were stories circulating in South Boston that he had been killed. So, Bulger ordered him home and made him stand in front of the liquor store for a few hours. That way everybody could see he was alive. Rakes feared Bulger so much he was willing to go through with the show.

Back at the L Street Bathhouse, Rakes thought about the day his livelihood, and to some extent his manhood, were taken from him. To protect his family, he allowed himself to be victimized by an extortion plot. His blood had been boiling for more than a decade when the authorities finally showed up to help. "I was called in to testify before the Grand Jury in

December of 1994," Rakes said. "Flemmi and Bulger found out about it and came up to me and told me I better tell the grand jury that they had taken my liquor store on the up and up—or else. I was scared to death, and I don't mind lying, so I went in and told the grand jury there was no extortion, no threats. Nothing."

Rakes figured he did what he was supposed to do, and that was confirmed a few hours after he left the grand jury when Bulger and Flemmi drove up next to him in South Boston. Rakes was walking when they pulled up to him in a car and thanked him for his testimony. But they also had to show off a little bit.

"Hey, why were they asking you questions about this other real estate deal?" Flemmi asked.

And just as Rakes began to answer, he looked down and saw that Flemmi was holding the transcript of his testimony that was supposed to be sealed and private.

"Can you believe that?" Rakes asked incredulously. "Those guys had the transcript. They knew I protected them, so I was safe, but Jesus!"

A few weeks after his first grand jury testimony, Rakes was approached by a U.S. District Attorney, who scolded him for blowing the case for them. Rakes was promised that if he went back in and gave truthful testimony, they would have Bulger, Flemmi, and Martorano arrested within two days. That was about forty-eight hours too long for Rakes's liking, but he agreed. He went back in to testify on Wednesday, and Flemmi was arrested the next day.

"But Bulger gets away," Rakes exclaimed. "Holy shit! He's the one I was really afraid of. So, now I'm sweating bullets."

And six months later, when he saw Bulger standing across the street with two hulking men he didn't recognize, Rakes was afraid of real bullets. So, he swam. And he swam. As fast as he could.

"I'd rather drown in the ocean than have that guy catch me," Rakes said.

His fear of Whitey Bulger was genuine and justified, and that fear would have served Debbie Davis well.

CHAPTER SIX

On the Banks of the Neponset River

On the day Steve Davis turned forty-three years old, he went to the beach. September 22, 2000, was an unseasonably warm 78 degrees in the Boston area, and most New Englanders celebrated the opportunity to steal an extra day of summer. Days like this were rare and to be appreciated. But despite the weather and the occasion of his birthday, Steve Davis was not in the mood for a celebration.

He stood on the shores of the Neponset River in Dorchester and looked out across the water. To the right of the magnificent Boston skyline was a partial view of the University of Massachusetts–Boston campus. Steve's gaze was prolonged as a flood of emotions raced through his mind. He felt sorrow and hope, longing and despair, and as he so often did, he felt rage. *Fucking Bulgers*, he thought.

Steve was standing right in the middle of a scene that only fate could have conjured. Eight days earlier, the body of Thomas King was found buried near the river's edge beneath the MBTA's Red Line bridge less than fifty yards from where Steve was now standing. Whitey Bulger was responsible for that.

And in eleven days, on October 3, 2000, presidential candidates Al Gore and George Bush would hold the first of three debates at UMASS-Boston. Billy Bulger was responsible for that.

Billy Bulger left the Massachusetts State Senate to become president of the University of Massachusetts in 1996. It was a great victory for him to bring the prestigious presidential debate to Boston, but it was an inconvenient truth that the press coverage leading up to the debate focused on his fugitive brother and the discovery of another one of his victim's bodies, and the continued search for another.

As Jim Lehrer of PBS opened the debate with, "Good evening from the Clark Athletic Center at the University of Massachusetts in Boston," police were still sifting through the soil looking for the body of Debbie Davis. It was a fruitless search at this point, because Kevin Weeks didn't know exactly where Debbie was buried. Weeks had been indicted in November 1999 on federal racketeering charges and was now cooperating with authorities. With pinpoint accuracy he had led them to the bodies of Barrett, McIntyre, and Hussey in January 2000. He helped investigators find Thomas King, but he was not especially helpful locating Debbie.

"I led them to where I thought Tommy King was buried," Weeks testified. "I didn't lead them to Debra Davis. I didn't know at the time where Debra Davis was buried. Again, I had nothing to do with her. I had no knowledge other than that they [Bulger and Flemmi] had killed her. But, you know, they [the investigators] must have somehow received other information or whatever, or just went there in the area and started digging all around until they found another body. I don't know how they came about it."

It may have been Flemmi himself who instructed investigators to continue their search along the banks of the Neponset, though it was Weeks who sat in a police trailer at the location for over a month. Or, it may simply have been an educated guess on the part of the investigators who by now had a firm belief that Flemmi had killed Debbie. They had even followed up on street rumors and searched the basement of the Marconi Club where some people thought Debbie was killed and buried. The police came away with nothing—except the same nagging suspicion that Debbie Davis had been killed and disposed of like so many other Bulger and Flemmi victims. That may explain why they persisted with the backhoe excavation searching for Debbie's body for five weeks. Extreme efforts were made. Nearly thirty members of the State Police, the medical examiner's office, and the DEA began searching each day at 7:00 a.m., and they went until dark. There were many long days in the cold and rain, but they continued searching while the Davis family continued hoping.

"When Kevin Weeks started to talk," Steve Davis recalls, "I didn't think he'd be talking about Debbie. I thought she was outside of all that. When it came out, I didn't think Bulger. Then again, I know he must have been excited to kill her, because my sister didn't like him."

Steve Davis and most of his family were on site for at least part of every day during the digging. When they were there, they huddled together drinking coffee, eating donuts, and feeling helpless. "It's been a month, Steve," Detective Daniel Doherty told him. "If they did bury your sister here, her body must have been swept away in the tides. We can't find her. We're sorry."

When the decision was made to suspend the search, Steve was disappointed, but not dissuaded. He pulled out his cell phone and made a call. The police easily overheard him ordering the delivery of a bulldozer. As soon as the police pulled up their stakes and moved out, Steve was moving in. He'd continue the digging himself.

"You can't do that," Doherty said. "This is a crime scene."

"It ain't a crime scene if you're leaving," Steve argued. "There's a whole empty spot right over there that you've left untouched."

Steve's bull mastiff puppy had been running to and from an area that still hadn't been excavated. Steve thought the dog was on to something. He planned to start digging right there. For their part, the police didn't want Steve doing any independent digging, but they weren't sure they could stop him, so they agreed to search for a few more days.

Thomas King's body was found on September 19. The remains of a second body weren't discovered until October 19. That body—later identified as Debbie Davis—was zipped inside a crimson colored body bag and taken away on a gurney. Looking across the water, Steve Davis could see the condominium where Whitey Bulger lived at the time of his sister's murder. It wasn't much more than a hundred yards away. "Fucking government," Davis said this time.

The picture, once so blurred, had finally come into full focus. It had taken nineteen years for the tale to unravel, but it was now clear to the Davis family: Whitey Bulger and Steve Flemmi had killed their sister and Olga's daughter, with the help and protection of the U.S. government. It was the now famous Wolf Hearings that convinced them of that.

As the case against Flemmi, Frank Salemme, and John Martorano went forward from the 1995 indictments, Flemmi kept quiet about his status as a top echelon informant for the

FBI. But in March 1997, the judge who had been assigned to the case found evidence implicating Flemmi as such. That judge, Mark L. Wolf, had a private meeting with Flemmi on April 16, 1997. Flemmi ultimately admitted he had been an FBI informant for thirty years, and the FBI confirmed it. The cat was out of the bag.

"Steve Flemmi told me that ain't nothing," Weeks testified. "He says 'Wait until the whole truth comes out. This ain't nothing.' I says, 'You're an informant! You're ratting on people?' He says, 'Wait until the whole story comes out before you decide.'"

Flemmi, Frank Salemme, and John Martorano were all residents of the Plymouth House of Corrections while the Wolf hearings were going on. It had to be an uncomfortable time for Flemmi who had suddenly been revealed as a rat. Martorano, who considered Bulger and Flemmi his best friends and made them his children's godfathers, would say later that it broke his heart to learn they were informants.

Martorano went right to work. While Flemmi argued his case should be dismissed because, as an informant, he believed he had immunity from prosecution, Martorano got the wheels spinning for a plea bargain. He had has brother, Jimmy Martorano, make a call to Tom Foley, the commander of Special Services for the Massachusetts State Police, who had been deeply involved in the Winter Hill Gang investigation since 1990. Foley and a few of his colleagues went to Jimmy Martorano's home and learned that while it was very important to John Martorano that he not be labeled as a rat, he was willing to spill his guts.

"A rat is a no good guy," Martorano says. "I was brought up to believe that's the worst person in the world. It's the opposite of the way I want to live." But he did it anyway. In fact, Martorano, who was charged with extortion and racketeering at the time of his arrest, blabbed on and on until he admitted to killing twenty people. "I wanted to tell the truth first," Martorano would say. "I figured if my story came out it would be a true story, and not somebody else's story."

He told the feds that his first murder victim was Tony Veranis in 1966. He claimed it was self-defense. Veranis was a tough guy, a boxer who got the better of Jimmy Martorano at an after-hours bar one night. John Martorano went to that same bar the next night. Veranis went up to him, perhaps to say "no hard feelings," but Martorano claims he pulled a gun on him, so he shot him in the head. He left with Veranis's limp body slumped over his shoulder and dumped it in the Blue Hills.

Martorano also claimed self-defense when he killed John "Touch" Bayno. Martorano didn't like the way Bayno was supposedly staring at him while he was on a date, so an argument ensued that spilled into a back alley. That's where Bayno, he says, pulled a knife on him. Martorano took the knife away and stabbed Bayno in the chest with it. He claims he put Bayno in his car for the sole purpose of bringing him to a hospital, but since Bayno wouldn't stop cursing at him and challenging him to a fight, Martorano stabbed him twenty more times, this time with his own knife. He dumped Bayno's body in an alley in the South End.

"Why stab him more?" Martorano was asked under oath years later.

"Cuz he wouldn't shut up."

He admitted to many more killings and shootings, some were innocent victims killed or wounded by mistake, others were specified hits at the direction of Bulger or Flemmi or both. He didn't kill for money or vengeance, he says; he did it out of loyalty for friends and family. "Family comes first,"

Martorano would testify. "My father taught me that. The priests and the nuns that I grew up with told me that. I always try to be a nice guy."

Of course, he failed to be nice more often than not. But he was successful in getting a plea agreement with the federal government before any of his criminal cohorts did. After admitting to participating in twenty murders and several other serious crimes, Martorano was sentenced to fourteen years in prison and served twelve. He's a free man today.

Kevin Weeks also decided to rat on the rat. He, like the Davis family, watched the whole story come out in dribs and drabs during the summer of 1997. First, they learned of Flemmi being an informant. In June they heard about the release of an affidavit in which Flemmi stated he and Bulger believed they had immunity from prosecution for any crimes short of murder.

That belief may have started earlier, but it was confirmed in April 1985, when Bulger and Flemmi went to FBI agent John Morris's home for dinner. John Connolly was there as well. The men were celebrating the foiling of a DEA investigation when Bulger found an electronic bug in his car. Bulger, ever the gracious guest, brought a bottle of wine and a bottle of champagne, and he heard Morris say, "You can do anything you want as long as you don't 'clip' anyone." Flemmi gave sworn testimony to that statement two decades later.

There were more stories. Flemmi installed a wire at a Mafia induction ceremony. Bulger and Flemmi infiltrated the headquarters of Jerry Angiulo at 98 Prince Street by offering the FBI schematics of the interior as well as information about the types of alarms and door locks that were at that location. Bulger met Morris in a Lechmere parking lot in Cambridge and told him everything he knew about the place. Later, Bulger

identified the men who robbed a Medford bank over Memorial
Day weekend in 1980, and Flemmi told the FBI about a Mafia
plan to kill a U.S. attorney.

These and other revelations came out slowly at first, and
then in one final surge when Judge Wolf concluded ten months
of hearings and released his 661-page decision in *United States
v. Salemme*. September 15, 1999 was the day that changed
everything. Wolf's findings confirmed what had been reported
about Bulger and Flemmi's relationship with the FBI, which
in turn, inspired Weeks to rescind any loyalty he felt toward
them, and ultimately led to the discovery of six bodies, including Debbie Davis's.

Judge Wolf let the world in on Flemmi and Bulger's dirty
little secrets. He identified Flemmi as the rat who told the FBI
where Salemme was hiding out after the Fitzgerald car bombing. Salemme was arrested while the charges against Flemmi
were dropped.

Judge Wolf revealed that Flemmi led the FBI to Joey
Barboza's killer in 1976, and that in October of 1980, Flemmi
and Bulger infiltrated Angiulo's headquarters at 98 Prince
Street which led to the convictions of Angiulo and much of the
leadership of the La Cosa Nostra (LCN) in Boston. Following
the success of that operation, Morris invited Connolly, Bulger,
and Flemmi back to his home for a celebration. Bulger and
Flemmi brought wine and a champagne bucket for Morris.
Morris gave Flemmi a painting from Korea. Later, additional
convictions against La Cosa Nostra members were secured
after Flemmi helped the FBI bug Vanessa's, a restaurant in the
Prudential Building owned by mafia soldier, Angelo "Sonny"
Mercurio. Flemmi drew a detailed diagram of the restaurant's
interior while Bulger watched, and they then handed it over to
FBI Special Agent John Connolly.

In addition to detailing how much Flemmi and Bulger had helped the FBI, Judge Wolf also exposed what the FBI had done for them. Connolly told them the Massachusetts State Police had bugged the Lancaster Street Garage, that George Kaufman's phone had been tapped as part of a DEA investigation targeting Bulger and Flemmi, and that a Boston police lieutenant would be wearing a wire when he met with Flemmi in 1988. And there was so much more.

Morris and Connolly also identified for Bulger and Flemmi "at least a dozen individuals who were either FBI informants or sources for other law enforcement agencies." One of those individuals was Brian Halloran, who was killed after Connolly told Bulger he was cooperating with the feds regarding the murder of a legitimate businessman named Roger Wheeler in Tulsa, Oklahoma. It was all part of a year-long killing spree that included several innocent victims, including Debbie Davis and Michael Donahue.

In 1981 Roger Wheeler was the owner of World Jai Alai, and unfortunately for him, he hired retired FBI special agent Paul Rico to be his head of security. Rico saw an opportunity for a big score. He teamed up with the president of World Jai Alai, Richard Donovan, and a man named John Callahan, who was a friend of John Martorano's and a wannabe gangster. Rico, Donovan, and Callahan wanted to buy World Jai Alai, and they offered Wheeler $50 million for it. Wheeler refused. That's all it took to get him killed. A plan was hatched and carried out. They would kill Wheeler and get his widow to sell.

Callahan talked to Martorano about taking Wheeler out, and Rico went directly to Flemmi. Unexpectedly, both Martorano and Flemmi expressed reservations, but both came on board when Callahan told Winter Hill that once he owned

World Jai Alai, he'd give them $10,000 a week for protection from the Mafia.

The roles were divided up. Rico followed Wheeler for a few weeks to study his routine. He gave that information to Callahan who passed it along to Martorano. Another Winter Hill member, Joe MacDonald, went to Tulsa to help. Flemmi put a package together that included a machine gun with a silencer, a grease gun, a .38 caliber pistol, and a ski mask. He put all these in a suitcase and loaded it onto a Trailways bus headed for Tulsa, Oklahoma, where Wheeler lived and Martorano was waiting.

Rico learned that on the morning of May 17, 1981, Wheeler had scheduled a tee time to play golf at the Southern Hills Country Club. Martorano, wearing a false beard, sunglasses, and a baseball cap, waited in a rental car in the parking lot for about thirty minutes when he saw Wheeler dressed in a dark pinstripe suit get into his car. Martorano got out of the rental and shot Wheeler between the eyes. Police photographs confirmed the accuracy of Martorano's aim and also show Wheeler sitting behind the wheel, slumped to his right, his head resting on a gym bag.

Callahan gave MacDonald and Martorano $25,000 each for the hit. Martorano kept $9,000 for himself and gave the rest to Bulger and Flemmi.

Wheeler was dead, and so was any deal to buy World Jai Alai because his widow also refused to sell. She was an innocent woman that Bulger and Flemmi chose to leave alone, but just four months after Wheeler was killed, another innocent woman was killed—Debbie Davis.

Flemmi and Bulger may have been especially concerned that Debbie could implicate them and reveal their relationship with the FBI, because the heat was on. By September 1981 when Debbie was killed, Bulger and Flemmi knew that Brian Halloran could take them down on the Wheeler shooting. Halloran was drinking buddies with Callahan, and was the first person Callahan offered the contract killing to. Halloran turned it down, but at a subsequent meeting Callahan gave him $20,000 anyway. "That's for your time," Callahan said. More likely, it was for his silence, but Halloran didn't keep quiet, and it appears that Bulger may have inadvertently inspired him to start talking.

A man named George Pappas was shot in the head while dining with Halloran and Frank Salemme's brother, Jackie, at the Four Seas Restaurant in downtown Boston. And in Bulger's informant file, Connolly wrote on October 15, 1981, that the source "advised that George Pappas was murdered by Brian Halloran who was high on coke."

Twelve days later, Bulger changed that story to say Jackie Salemme killed Pappas. Bulger switched back to claim it was, in fact, Halloran who pulled the trigger, but the Mafia still wanted Halloran "hit in the head" to prevent him from testifying against Jackie Salemme. Flemmi's informant file includes the following assertion: "The Mafia continues to hideout Jackie Salemme until they can line up Brian Halloran to be taken out. Halloran walked in on the Angiulos recently and asked why they wanted to 'hit' him. They were dumbfounded, but were afraid to say anything or make any moves because they suspected that the law may have wired him up."

So, in part, because Bulger and Flemmi had pointed a finger at him, Halloran was charged in the Pappas murder. Halloran was squeezed into a position where his best option may have been to roll over on Winter Hill.

There were at least two attempts on Halloran's life. After the second one, he went to the FBI. On January 5, 1982, he explained to agents Leo Brunnick and Joe Montanari that he feared for his own life, and for the safety of his wife and infant child. Halloran was immediately opened as an FBI informant.

Brunnick and Montanari met with Halloran dozens of times over the next three months. Halloran admitted to them that he'd been involved in several murders with the Winter Hill Gang, but Brunnick and Montanari didn't pursue those cases. Halloran was yet another known murderer who wouldn't be investigated. The FBI didn't want his conviction. They wanted his information. Halloran told them he would be willing to testify against Bulger, Flemmi, and Callahan, and that he'd be willing to wear a wire.

In late April, Brunnick talked to his supervisor, John Morris, about the plans to put a wire on Halloran when he met with Callahan at the Paddock Restaurant in Somerville. Brunnick needed Morris to approve a surveillance and security team. It was the first Morris had heard of Halloran's cooperation. He took the information to John Connolly. "It was bad judgment," Morris says. "Because it placed Connolly in a difficult situation. I should have known he would report that back to Bulger and Flemmi."

Connolly did let them know, and two weeks later on May 11, 1982, Halloran was killed along the South Boston waterfront in broad daylight. Dozens of people scattered and ducked for cover as Bulger and an unidentified masked man fired dozens of machine gun bullets into a small Datsun. When the shooting finally stopped, Halloran was dead, and so was another man named Michael Donahue. He was collateral damage in Bulger's war against anyone who would try to bring him down.

At 5:45 in the afternoon, Michael Donahue called his wife, Patricia, to say he was on his way home, but first he was going to give a friend a ride. That friend was Brian Halloran, a fellow member of the Teamsters Union.

Halloran was at the Pier Grill Restaurant off Seaport Boulevard. Unbeknownst to him, Kevin Weeks was in a nearby parking lot watching him through binoculars. When Halloran got up to leave, Weeks called Bulger on a two-way radio and said, "The balloon is rising." That was a coded reference to Halloran whose oversized skull had earned him the nickname, "Balloon Head."

Donahue pulled up in the Datsun. Halloran got in, and within seconds Bulger pulled up alongside in his 1975 Malibu. Bulger was wearing a mustache and wig that made him look like a Winter Hill Gang associate named Jimmy Flynn.

"Brian!" Bulger shouted. Halloran looked up and thought he saw Jimmy Flynn, and then the bullets started flying. Donahue was hit four times and killed instantly when one bullet pierced the left side of his brain, but Halloran managed to get out of the car. It was not a good idea.

"As he walked toward the rear of his vehicle," Weeks testified, "Jim Bulger just started shooting right at him. Brian Halloran went down and Jim Bulger just kept shooting him. His body was bouncing on the ground."

Despite twenty-two gunshot wounds, Halloran lived long enough to mistakenly tell police that Flynn was the shooter. Flynn was arrested and charged, but later acquitted.

Meanwhile, minutes after the shooting, Patricia Donahue was preparing dinner for Michael and their three young children. When the 6:00 news came on and described a gangland slaying, she recognized the family car. She became frantic and started hyperventilating. When she finally got her breathing under control, she called the police and every hospital in Boston, but she was given no answers. "Hours later," Patricia says, "it seemed like an eternity, the police finally came and took me to the hospital. He had already died."

Bulger left the shooting and went to get a bite to eat at the home of his long-time girlfriend, Theresa Stanley. Weeks swears that Bulger met Morris and Connolly there, and while the three men shared some Beck's beer, Morris told Bulger that an FBI agent watching Halloran had seen the hit go down, and had gotten the license plate number of Bulger's car. Once he knew the police were looking for the car, Bulger had it taken apart in a garage, and the feds never found it.

"Thank God for Beck's beer," Bulger toasted.

Perhaps at the same time Patricia learned her husband was dead, Bulger and Weeks returned to the murder scene to pick up a hubcap that had fallen off Bulger's car. They then drove the short distance to Flemmi's mother's house on East Third Street where they told Flemmi the story. Weeks, who initially thought Flemmi might have been the masked man in the backseat, was surprised to hear Flemmi say he wished he were there. After dinner, Weeks took the guns that were used over to Marina Bay and threw them into the ocean.

The next day, Flemmi and Pat Nee were walking on the beach when Nee admitted his part in the Halloran and Donahue shooting, lamenting the fact that his gun had jammed.

That same day, Connolly filed a report claiming the wise-guys in Charlestown had learned Halloran was giving information to the State Police through Halloran's brother, Robert, who happened to be a state trooper. It was a false report. All Brian had told Robert was that his life was in danger.

"He told me Whitey and Stevie were trying to set him up like they did to Tommy King," Robert says.

Bulger's FBI file indicates that ten days later he told Connolly that "Jimmy Flynn did the hit on Halloran with Jimmy McCormick from Charlestown as wheelman. Pat Flannery, Billy Coyman, and Red Noonan were in the back-up van near the scene."

Bulger and Connolly concocted another elaborate tale about Flannery wanting Halloran dead, because he knew too much about a murder in Canada. The only truth in their report was the fact that the weapons used to kill Halloran and Donahue were tossed in the ocean, but they added that McCormick was bragging about being involved in the hit, which was a lie.

And in July, Connolly reported that Bulger didn't know Halloran was cooperating with the feds until he read about it in the newspaper after Halloran's death. That was also a lie.

Of course, there remained another loose end. John Callahan needed to go. The Oklahoma police were focusing on Callahan, and Bulger and Flemmi believed Callahan would fold under questioning. So, Bulger told Martorano that he had killed Halloran specifically for him. Halloran knew who the trigger man was, and Bulger got him to shut up.

"But Callahan's a good friend of mine," Martorano protested. "I don't want to kill a friend."

"Hey, he ratted on you," Bulger reminded Martorano. "He told Halloran you killed Wheeler."

Martorano relented pretty quickly. "I felt lousy, but you know these were my partners," Martorano says. "We were up to our necks in murders already."

The next one took place at the Fort Lauderdale Airport in August 1982. It was much more convenient for Martorano, who had been living in Florida since early 1979 when he left Massachusetts to evade a race-fixing indictment. He brought his eighteen-year-old girlfriend with him. Martorano was thirty-five when he started dating fifteen-year-old Patricia Lytle, and when it was time to go on the run, he told her they were going on a vacation. "We ended up staying for sixteen years," Patricia said. While they were there, Martorano and Patricia had a son, James, whose godfather is Whitey Bulger. Before James was born, Martorano killed his friend John Callahan.

Martorano and Callahan met at the airport, shaking hands and exchanging pleasantries. Martorano graciously took Callahan's briefcase and put it in the back of his van. Callahan got in front, and Martorano got in the backseat, pulled a pistol out from under a white towel, and shot his friend in the back of the head.

Joe MacDonald pulled up in another car and began to help with the plan to make it appear as though Callahan had been killed by a group of Cubans in a drug deal gone awry. They put Callahan's body in the trunk of MacDonald's car and drove it to the Miami International Airport. Along the way, MacDonald thought he heard a moan coming from the trunk, so they pulled over so MacDonald could shoot Callahan a few more times. They were once again on their way. They left the car at the Miami airport, and dropped Callahan's wallet and briefcase near some Cuban bars in downtown Miami. Bulger, known for disposing of bodies in secret burial sites, thought Martorano should have hidden Callahan's body in an unmarked grave. "He should have gotten off his fat ass," Flemmi claims Bulger said. "There's a lot of sand down there."

Despite knowing who was responsible for the Wheeler and Callahan murders, Connolly filed a written report that stated he just happened to call Bulger on the day of Wheeler's murder and that they had both seen a television news report about it. Bulger speculated it was "probably a couple of guys trying to kidnap Wheeler for a ransom, and he fought them off." Furthermore, Connolly offered the alibi that Bulger was staying at the Chateau Great Western motel in Provincetown "with female companionship" when Callahan was killed.

And thus, an unholy alliance had been formed. Morris and Connolly had crossed a line from which there was no turning back. They knew with great certainty that Bulger and Flemmi were responsible for the murders of Wheeler, Halloran, and Callahan. And when Flemmi's girlfriend, Debbie Davis, went missing in the middle of this killing spree, two experienced FBI agents would have to presume at the very least that Flemmi was involved. Yet, they did nothing. "We knew who these guys were," Connolly would later say. "They did not have a paper route when we first met them. All of the top echelon informants are murderers. The government put me in business with murderers."

Morris was in that business as well. He entered it willingly and with his hand extended for payoffs, but he may have exited with intense internal conflict. His greed, pride, and ego prevented him from exposing Bulger and Flemmi and thereby exposing himself, but he claims to have tried to rein them in. He says he tried to get Bulger and Flemmi closed as informants. And he says he stopped them from killing a bookie named John Bahorian.

During a 1988 investigation of alleged payoffs to members of the Boston Police Department, it was discovered that Bahorian was making payments to Flemmi. Both of them were targeted for wiretaps by the investigators. Morris knew that electronic surveillance could lead to Flemmi's arrest, and that Flemmi could save himself by revealing the nature of his relationship with Morris. Even so, Morris says he told Flemmi and Bulger to leave Bahorian alone, because he didn't "want another Halloran."

Testifying to that fact more than once, Morris was acknowledging that he knew Bulger and Flemmi killed Halloran. Morris, Connolly, Rico, and probably others knew Bulger and Flemmi were multiple murderers, but they never did anything to stop them. In fact, they consistently impeded investigations, lied in reports, and informed Bulger and Flemmi any time legitimate investigations were getting close to nailing them.

Morris went so far as to ask Bulger for money less than a month after Halloran was killed. Morris was sent to Glen Cove, Georgia, for a drug training seminar, and upon his arrival, he realized the surrounding community was a vacation resort. He wanted his secretary, Debra Noseworthy, with whom he was having an affair, to come down for a romantic getaway. So, he asked Connolly if Bulger would pay for an airline ticket for her. Bulger obliged with a $1,000 first class ticket.

Morris liked the way this relationship worked. He kept his mouth shut and occasionally got nice things. For cooking and serving dinner to Bulger, Flemmi, and Connolly at his Lexington home one night, Morris received $5,000. Bulger pulled an envelope full of cash out of the breast pocket of his leather jacket before leaving. Morris thought for a moment about giving it back, but then he thought better of it.

Bulger also gave Morris a case of expensive imported wine once, and when Morris opened it, he found a thousand dollars in cash stuffed in between the bottles. He kept the money, and drank the wine. Morris drank a lot of wine. And he drank a bit too much while meeting with Bulger and Flemmi at the Hotel Colonade one night in April 1981. No worries, though. Bulger drove him home.

Throughout the years, the special relationship Bulger had with the FBI—the one that was supposed to be strictly business—evolved into quite a social relationship. Morris recalls going to Flemmi's parents' home for dinner in the fall of 1983. Connolly, Bulger, Flemmi, and Flemmi's parents were all there, and for a time, so was Billy Bulger. As was his custom, Billy simply walked in as if he owned the place. He was there to watch TV, but the then senate president became clearly uncomfortable when he saw two FBI agents socializing with his brother. So, he walked through the social gathering without so much as a word and parked himself in front of a TV in another room. An hour later, he got up and left.

Billy Bulger encountered a similar situation at that house when it was Connolly and FBI special agent, Jim Ring, meeting with Bulger and Flemmi. That was the meeting at which Flemmi drew the diagram of Vanessa's Restaurant. Again, Billy Bulger watched his TV program and left without uttering a peep.

Now, if Morris is to be believed, he eventually felt enough contrition to try to stop Bulger and Flemmi by exposing them as informants. He figured that was the only way to stop their unrestricted criminal and violent behavior. He told reporter Gerald O'Neill of the *Boston Globe* about his special relationship with Bulger and Flemmi, and O'Neill published the story on September 20, 1988. Morris hoped that the La Cosa Nostra would kill Bulger and Flemmi as soon as the story came out. "They've outlived their usefulness," Morris said at the time.

But the Mafia spared Bulger, and Bulger spared Morris, despite knowing that Morris leaked his informant status to the *Globe*. It was October 1995, ten months after Bulger fled from his indictment, when Morris received a call in his office from a man identifying himself as "Mr. White," but Morris recognized the voice immediately. "I want you to use your Machiavellian mind to contact your sources at the *Globe*," Bulger began. "You get them to retract the story about me being an informant. Remember you took money from me, and if I'm going to jail, you're coming with me."

Bulger reminded Morris about the case of wine and the thousand dollars he had given him, and then hung up abruptly. Morris was frightened, both for his safety and his job. The health issues he was already dealing with worsened. Within weeks, he checked into Massachusetts General Hospital for tests, and while he was there he went into full cardiac and respiratory arrest. Morris retired from the FBI a month later.

Some, but not all of this was recounted in the report issued by Judge Wolf. After hearing the testimony of forty-six witnesses over eighty days, Judge Wolf had to come up with a finding of facts. It was incumbent upon him to discern what and who was believable, especially when so much of the testimony was contradicted.

Anyone who read Wolf's report also learned that when Bulger fled in 1995, an agent named Charles Gianturco was put in charge of finding him. And that it just so happened that in 1978, in his role as an informant, Bulger had told Connolly about a plan to kill Gianturco's brother, Nick. In effect, Bulger saved Nick Gianturco's life and later dined with Nick, and exchanged gifts with him. So, Charles Gianturco may not have been the best choice to lead the investigation into finding Bulger. Clearly, the effort to find him lacked urgency.

Wolf wrote about Bulger's return to Boston in late January of 1995 when he was exchanging one girlfriend for another. He dropped off his longtime companion, Theresa Stanley, who had decided not to go on the run with him, and he picked up his other lady friend, Catherine Greig, instead. Despite knowing this, the FBI didn't get around to interviewing Stanley for over fifteen months. Any information she was able to provide at that time was deemed in an FBI report to be "dated and of diminished value."

Connolly wasn't interviewed about Bulger's whereabouts until two years after Bulger disappeared. He told Charles Gianturco that Morris had once told Bulger and Flemmi "that they were so good, he could get them off for anything short of murder." But Gianturco did not include that in his report.

Finally, in August 1999, the FBI placed Bulger on its list of Ten Most Wanted fugitives. A month later, Wolf's report was released, and everyone, including the Davis family, began to realize the magnitude of the FBI's corrupt relationship with two of Boston's most notorious criminals. This was part of the slow reveal. First, the corruption is uncovered, then the bodies are.

"If Bulger is going to be apprehended, it will be because of these bodies," Jack Levin, a professor of sociology and criminology at Northeastern University told *ABC News.* "Now there's evidence of mass murder. And mass murder of not only crime figures, but ordinary people." And once the bodies were found, every word of the Wolf report could be dissected and analyzed and ultimately used against the U.S. government in some kind of wrongful death suit. In his report, Wolf wrote the following about the value and the danger of using informants:

> Informants are valuable, if not vital, assets in combatting serious crime. The government's ability to promise an informant confidentiality is often important to securing his cooperation and protecting his safety. In recognition of this, the FBI has historically been permitted to operate its sources in secret, even from officials of the Department of Justice.
>
> However, as Attorney General Harlan Fiske Stone, who later became the Chief Justice of the United States, warned in 1924, when he established the FBI: "There is always the possibility that a secret police may become a menace to free government and free institutions because it carries with it the possibility of abuses of power which are not always quickly apprehended or understood."

Wolf provided some history regarding how the FBI developed its guidelines for the use of informants, and that those guidelines directed the "FBI not take any action to conceal a crime by one of its informants." Furthermore, if the FBI did learn about a serious crime committed by one of its informants, "the Bureau was directed to inform the Department of Justice," and the Department would make a determination about whether to keep the informant or close him and investigate with the intention of prosecuting him.

"The evidence in this case," Wolf concluded, "indicates that the Attorney General's Guidelines were routinely ignored with regard to top echelon informants generally. As the government acknowledges, it is clear that they were regularly disregarded concerning Bulger and Flemmi."

And that evidence gave the Debbie Davis's family, and others, the right to file a wrongful death suit.

CHAPTER SEVEN

Davis v. Government

Flemmi and Bulger were indicted for murdering Debbie Davis in November 2000. The Davis's lawsuit against the government was filed on September 17, 2001, the twentieth anniversary of Debbie's death. There were the typical family meetings and predictable arguments about whether or not to file suit. Some of the siblings worried about the expense of suing and the prospect of losing. Others favored a fight for justice no matter the outcome. And still others considered the possibility of a pot of gold at the end of the rainbow. Ultimately, Debbie's brother Victor's persistence won out. He was the driving force behind it, and he was able to convince Olga to get the case into the courts just in the nick of time.

A major portion of the case was devoted to the ticking clock and the statute of limitations. That clock started ticking the moment the Davises could reasonably have known that Flemmi and Bulger killed Debbie, and that the FBI was partially responsible do to negligence. When did the Davises have enough pieces of the puzzle to figure out that the FBI's corruption directly or indirectly led to Debbie's death? Well, it couldn't have been before they knew for sure that Debbie was dead. Despite having their suspicions about Flemmi, there was no proof, no charges, and no body. Until that was discovered, Olga and her children could reasonably continue to hope that Debbie was alive and well somewhere.

"An investigation by the Davis family before Weeks's cooperation would not have revealed that Davis was murdered, or that Bulger and Flemmi were responsible," Judge William G. Young correctly stated during the Davis family's trial against the government. "Flemmi denied it. Davis might have had personal reasons to run away. She had been removed from the missing persons database . . . the Davis family had no sufficient knowledge of the factual basis of their claim." Additionally, even if the Davis's knew or assumed Debbie was dead, that didn't implicate the FBI. "So, we have to ask when would a reasonable person have known that the FBI arguably had a hand in the Davis murder?" Judge Young asked and then answered, "It doesn't seem until Weeks gives his testimony."

The relevant facts for determining the timeframe for the statute of limitations were these: Weeks was arrested on November 17, 1999. He began cooperating with law enforcement in December 1999. The public wasn't notified of that cooperation until the bodies of John McIntyre, Bucky Barrett, and Deborah Hussey were discovered on January 14, 2000.

Imprecisely, that's when the clock started ticking. By then the Wolf decision had revealed the corrupt relationship between the FBI and Bulger and Flemmi. So, when Weeks pointed to where the bodies were buried, thus pointing a finger at Bulger and Flemmi as the murderers, the judge determined that's when the victims' families could start putting two and two together.

The Davises could have had more time because Debbie's body wasn't found for another ten months, but they chose to file their suit along with the Husseys and Litifs. Still, the families had two years to notify the FBI of their intentions to sue and their letter dated September 17, 2001 beat the clock by as many as four months. "So the statute of limitations is satisfied," the judge concluded.

With that matter resolved, the Davis, Hussey, and Litif lawsuit proceeded with the primary claim of government liability based on three related theories: 1) that the special relationship the FBI forged with Flemmi and Bulger brought with it an obligation to control them; 2) that the FBI created a dangerous condition and should have realized Bulger and Flemmi were likely to cause physical harm to other people; and 3) that the FBI's own involvement in murders and other serious crimes were enabling Bulger and Flemmi to potentially do more harm to people like Debbie Davis.

By now it would seem to have been easy to connect these dots, but the strength of the families' case was weakened by the concept of foreseeability. Should the government have been able to predict and, therefore, prevent the murder of someone like Debbie Davis? Furthermore, did the government have a duty to protect everyone in Bulger and Flemmi's zone of danger?

"The FBI should have known that Bulger was a vicious killer who did not hesitate to kill anyone who could harm him," attorney Michael J. Heineman argued while representing the estate of Debra Davis. And then he went further, "Debra Davis was such a person." Heineman put forth the argument that Debbie could have hurt Bulger by exposing him and Flemmi as FBI informants. His argument was circumstantial, but persuasive.

Heineman noted that Flemmi and Connolly were in regular contact with each other around the time of Debbie's disappearance, and that Bulger was in contact with Connolly two days before the murder. He also claimed that Flemmi told Bulger that Debbie had threatened to expose them. This claim was tough to prove, but he could prove that Flemmi met with Connolly the day after the murder. Heineman was able to affirm that Olga met with the FBI several times, but the agents never took notes or wrote any reports, and that "the FBI admitted going to the Randolph police station and obtaining the missing persons report, and the FBI claims now, not to possess that report." This did not cast the FBI in the best light.

There were also photos of Debbie obtained by the FBI that no longer existed. There was evidence and testimony that the FBI met with Olga several times but focused on what she knew about Flemmi rather than on the whereabouts of her daughter. When Olga accused them of not doing enough to find her daughter, "the FBI agents told Olga that Bulger and Flemmi knew people in funeral parlors and that they could dispose of bodies in dumpsters in green bags."

Clearly, Heineman argued, "This investigation was off the books." And the conversations with Olga were done exclusively to find out if Debbie had told any of her family members what she knew about Bulger and Flemmi's special relationship with the FBI. Having laid this foundation, Heineman took his argument a giant step forward when he stated, "The plaintiff respectfully suggests that the murder of Richard Castucci in 1976 literally paved the way for the murder of Debra Davis in 1981."

Castucci owned the Ebony nightclub in Revere, Massachusetts. He was also a bookmaker who later became a top echelon informant for the FBI. His demise came soon after he tipped the FBI off about the Winter Hill Gang's gambling activities and its safehouse in New York City. Castucci gave the information to his handler, Special Agent Tom Daly of the FBI, but it was likely Morris or Connolly who told Bulger and Flemmi about Castucci. Special agent Daly's last contact with Castucci was December 27, 1976. Three days later, Castucci's body was found with a bullet hole in the back of his head.

"The reason he was killed," Flemmi testified, "was because of giving up the apartment in New York where Joe MacDonald and Jimmy Sims were staying."

In April of 1976, Joe and Jimmy were fugitives and associates of the Winter Hill Gang. They were wanted for two armed robberies of rare stamps, and for the subsequent murder and attempted murder that took place. Soon after the robberies, MacDonald went to California and successfully shot and killed a potential witness against him named Raymond Lundgren. He then joined Sims at the safe house that John Martorano had secured for them in Greenwich Village, New York. The rent for the apartment was $1,000 a month, and it was pre-paid for one year by Winter Hill. Martorano also gave MacDonald and Sims $14,000 to hold them over until things cooled down.

While Joey Mac and Sims were in hiding, Connolly learned that another witness to the robberies, a man named Michael Kerzner, was cooperating with the FBI. Connolly told Bulger, who thought the best thing to do was to kill Kerzner.

On December 10, 1976, Bulger drove along the Massachusetts Turnpike with Flemmi in the passenger seat. They pulled up next to Kerzner, and Flemmi got off one shot, hitting Kerzner in the shoulder. Flemmi's gun jammed, and he was unable to get off another shot. Kerzner pulled off to the side of the road and survived the shooting, but he chose not to testify.

Castucci remained a threat to everyone involved. Bulger and Flemmi also owed Castucci $130,000, which ironically was not a factor in his killing. "That was a collateral gambling benefit," Flemmi said with a sly grin from the witness stand.

Castucci was sitting at a kitchen table counting a bag full of money when Martorano came in, walked behind him, and shot him in the back of the head. "After that, we had to clean it up," Martorano says matter-of-factly. "Stevie and Whitey cleaned it up. We had a sleeping bag and put Richie Castucci in the bag." Castucci was thrown into the trunk of a car, and that unregistered car was simply left abandoned in Revere.

Now, what did this have to do with the Davis family and their case? Because, Heineman argued, "If Bulger and Flemmi could murder a top echelon informant with the blessing of Agent Connolly, what fear could they possibly have in 1981 when they decided to murder Debra Davis who was a threat to expose their corrupt relationship with the FBI?" Heineman continued, "Nothing could be more telling of their fearlessness than the fact that Flemmi met with Agent Connolly on September 18, 1981, the day after he and Bulger killed Debra Davis. The FBI knew, or in the exercise of reasonable care, should have known that they had created these criminal monsters and, therefore was under a duty to exercise reasonable care to prevent further carnage. They did not, and Debra Davis and others died."

If the path to Debbie's murder didn't start with the Castucci murder, it could have begun at various points along the way, such as the 1967 murder of William Bennett, or the 1968 bombing of attorney John Fitzgerald's car. That's when FBI Special Agent Paul Rico set the wheels in motion for several decades of mayhem by tipping off Flemmi to impending indictments and allowing him to flee. Or, the path could have started in 1970 when the Las Vegas police complained that the FBI was interfering in its investigation of Flemmi in the murder of Peter Poulos. Or, it could have started in 1974 when Rico got the charges against Flemmi dropped and told him it was safe to come home, or later in 1974 when the FBI arranged for Flemmi and Bulger to meet at a Newton coffee shop. Or, it could have started in 1977 when the FBI learned that Flemmi made death threats against a man named Francis Green who owed him money, or in 1979 when the Boston Organized Crime Strike Force prosecutor, Jeremiah O'Sullivan, knew that Flemmi and Bulger were involved in a horse race-fixing scheme, but decided not to prosecute them, because Special Agents Morris and Connolly explained to O'Sullivan that Flemmi and Bulger were vital to them as an informants. O'Sullivan later testified he actually knew Flemmi was a murderer, but used "prosecutorial discretion" in deciding not to prosecute him.

O'Sullivan would claim Flemmi wasn't part of the original scheme, only that he received proceeds from it after the fact. That was a lie. O'Sullivan's own memorandum indicated that Bulger and Flemmi met to discuss the scheme, and that "Flemmi appeared to be a part of the core working group of the conspiracy." When confronted with that memorandum, O'Sullivan simply stated, "You've got me."

As for that crooked path that led to Debbie Davis's death, it was the Wolf hearings and subsequently the House Committee on Government Reform that concluded the real starting point was the 1965 murder of Eddie Deegan. It would seem, by this account, that Debbie Davis was murdered because of something that happened sixteen years before her death.

"Everything Secret Degenerates: The FBI's Use of Murders as Informants" was the title of the House Committee report released on February 3, 2004. It began with the summary conclusion that "known killers were protected from the consequences of their crimes and purposefully kept on the streets." And that began on March 12, 1965 when Eddie Deegan was found killed—gangland style—in an alleyway in Chelsea, Massachusetts.

Field memos from Boston FBI agents show they had a heads up that Deegan might be killed. They had microphone surveillance telling them Steve Flemmi's brother, Jimmy, had asked New England Mafia boss Raymond Patriarca for permission to kill Deegan because Deegan was "an arrogant, nasty sneak who should be killed." The memos even detailed Jerry Angiulo's admonishment of Jimmy for not using common sense when it came to killing people. That memo was filed two days before Deegan was shot in the back of the head. Nothing was done to prevent Deegan's murder.

A memo from Boston agents to the office of the FBI director, J. Edgar Hoover, a week after the killing stated:

> Informants report that Ronald Casessa [misspelling of Cassesso], Romeo Martin, Vincent "Jimmy" Flemmi and Joseph Barboza, prominent local hoodlums, were responsible for the killing. They accomplished this by having Roy French, another Boston hoodlum, set Deegan up in a proposed "breaking & entering" in Chelsea, Mass. French apparently walked in behind Deegan when they were gaining entrance to the building and fired the first shot hitting Deegan in the back of the head. Casessa and Martin immediately thereafter shot Deegan from the front. Anthony Stathopoulos was also in on the burglary but had remained outside in the car. When Flemmi and Barboza walked over to Stathopoulos's car, Stathopoulos thought it was the law and took off. Flemmi and Barboza were going to kill Stathopoulos also.

So, it would seem that despite the fact that the FBI knew who did it, because they (especially FBI Special Agent H. Paul Rico) were developing the Flemmi brothers as informants against Patriarca and Angiulo, they withheld evidence and allowed—even encouraged—Barboza to give false testimony leading to the conviction of four innocent men. Two died in prison, and the other two spent more than thirty years in jail.

"Furthermore," the House Committee reported, "federal officials appear to have taken affirmative steps to ensure that the individuals convicted would not obtain post-conviction relief and that they would die in prison."

The slope wasn't just slippery, it became an avalanche of ice when a memo to the Justice Department written in February 1970 stated that Barboza was threatening to retract his testimony and go to the press with the truth if the government didn't start to "provide him with sufficient money." The memo recommended that the government accede to the demands or the recent conviction of Patriarca might be overturned and result in "protracted and acrimonious litigation."

It took nearly forty years, but finally in 2007, a judge ordered the government to pay the families of the innocent men just over a $100 million. Three years after that, the bill was paid.

The FBI's association with Vincent "Jimmy the Bear" Flemmi has set a precedent for their similarly symbiotic relationship with the FBI for Stevie Flemmi and Whitey Bulger as the House report pointed out:

> There is no evidence that anyone expressed concern that Jimmy Flemmi would kill people while serving as a government informant. This is consistent with what happened

later when agents in the FBI's Boston office used Stephen Flemmi and James Bulger—who appear to have been involved in at least nineteen homicides—as informants for nearly a quarter of a century. Evidence obtained by the Committee leaves no doubt that at least some law enforcement personnel, including officials in FBI Director Hoover's office, were well aware that federal informants were committing murders.

The more crimes Bulger and Flemmi committed, and the more the FBI either knew about or facilitated or participated in those crimes, the more the FBI may have felt it had the upperhand, as demonstrated by one particular incident. Tony Ciulla, Billy Barnoski, and Jimmy Sousa had come up with a horse race fixing scheme in which they bribed jockeys to hold their horses back, and they'd simply bet on the other horses. When this was discovered by law enforcement officers, twenty-one people were indicted, but not Flemmi and Bulger. Knowing what might happen if Ciulla started cooperating with the feds, Connolly made Flemmi and Bulger promise not kill Ciulla.

"We had to give our assurances that that wouldn't happen," Flemmi testified.

This was pretty damning testimony, because it proved that Connolly could control Bulger and Flemmi when and if he wanted to. The implication was just as damning, because when Connolly said specifically, "Don't kill Ciulla," he was leaving the door open to kill others.

"The FBI could and did easily foresee that Bulger and Flemmi would kill again," Judge Young said. "Debra Davis was the next, although not the last, foreseeable victim."

But, in fact, their next victim was Sousa. Connolly never said they couldn't kill him. So, they did. Sousa was involved in another scheme to rob a dentist by getting him to buy fake gold. When Sousa was arrested, Winter Hill was concerned he would cave under police questioning. Sousa was summoned to Howie Winter's garage at 14 Marshall Street in Somerville.

Sousa arrived thinking he was going to be given money to pay for an attorney. Instead, John Martorano walked in and shot him in the head.

"I come in and he was bleeding a lot," Flemmi admits. "I put a can under him because the blood was falling on the floor, and we had to clean it up." Flemmi put Sousa's body in a car and brought it out to a wooded area in Boxford where Howie Winter had previously dug a hole. Sousa's body has never been found.

Judge Young began to describe Bulger and Flemmi as "mad dogs." In his view, an owner may not know if his rabid dog is going to bite, but he has a duty to stop the dog from running about. "But in this case," U.S. Attorney Lawrence Eiser argued, "it would be as if the people who owned the dog or lived with the dog were saying 'the dog bit me.' Because even after the FBI is on notice that Flemmi's killing people, the last person that would be foreseeable would be his own family. I mean, you don't kill anybody's family that's got thirty-three people."

"There's something to that," the judge responded.

And it mattered to the judge why Debbie Davis was killed. If it was because her romantic entanglement with Flemmi was coming to an end, her death may have been less foreseeable. That's why Heineman argued that the evidence suggested she was killed because she knew too much:

There's no other reason in the world for Bulger to be at that killing, in an empty house that's going to be moved into by Flemmi's mother. They have pliers with them. They have duct tape with them. And Whitey Bulger's there. I would suggest that's inconsistent with the rage killing, a romantic killing. She was grabbed when she entered the house as Flemmi said. She was questioned by Bulger. Something was said. Kiss on the forehead. You're going to a better place, or let her pray. But something was said during the time that she was alive and conscious and knew she was never coming out of the basement.

Heineman raised the single most significant question: Why was Bulger there? And here's another: Why was Bulger the one who killed her? She was Flemmi's girlfriend, and it was Flemmi's parents' house. Flemmi brought her there. He walked in behind her. What did he need Bulger for? Bulger's a cold-blooded killer, but Debbie Davis was not his problem. Or was she?

It's possible that Bulger killed Debbie as a favor to Flemmi. Maybe Flemmi had feelings for her, and just couldn't bring himself to do it. It's also possible Bulger killed her because she could expose him as an informant. Or, maybe Bulger just likes choking the life out of someone. And maybe Bulger didn't do it. There's reason to doubt anything and everything that Flemmi says.

Judge Young's opinion was that Flemmi had done it:

I reject any suggestion that her knowledge of his informant status with Connolly played any role in her death. It did not. In his warped mind that may be some justification, but those are the vapid maunderings of a vile and evil old man. He had her killed because their relationship was coming to an end he feared she would leave him for a younger person. When you have a murder of a woman by a man and they know each other, the man out of some misplaced view of ownership kills her because of a sexual attachment. Flemmi is not special. He's not some gangster in pursuit of his mob obligations. He's a pathetic, abusive murderer.

And Debbie Davis should have known that—or so the government argued. Trying very hard not to say "she was asking for it," Eiser argued that if the FBI had a duty to protect people from Flemmi, because it knew of his violent propensities, then anyone who also knew of his violence had a duty to protect themselves. But if the FBI hadn't been so grossly corrupt and complicit in Bulger and Flemmi's criminal behavior, it might have been a persuasive argument. Instead, the court concluded that under Massachusetts law, if an individual acted as the FBI agents had, that person would be liable. Therefore, the agents and, by association, the FBI were liable. In his ruling, Judge Young stated:

> Here, the government—our government—seriously argued that the horrifying acts of its agents against our own people fell within their legitimate "discretion," and that the victims and their families were somehow complicit in their own murders, well knowing no Commonwealth court has ever suggested such a bizarre legal theory. Most repulsive, the government—our government—virtually argued "she was asking for it," until the Court . . . warned them to steer clear.
>
> Most important, though, the government almost got away with it.
>
> This outcome was not inevitable. Judicial independence is not immutable, even in America. . . . Here's the partial bill: a criminal FBI agent, corrupt to the core, living in honorable retirement on a public pension; a half

dozen unsolved murders; literally dozens of people tortuously injured yet denied justice; two innocent men dying in prison under life sentences hopeless and helpless; others languishing in prison for years, three initially sentenced to death; two murdered young women lying in unmarked and forgotten graves. Think about that cost. I do.

The court ruled on January 29, 2010 in favor of the plaintiff and awarded the Estate of Debra Davis $1 million for loss of consortium, another $350,000 for conscious pain and suffering, and $2,005.60 for funeral expenses. The ruling was upheld on appeal. And each of the surviving Davis siblings received a check in the spring of 2012 for $187,000. It reminded Steve Davis of Whitey Bulger's question to him more than thirty years earlier: What's your life worth?

The other victims' families also won their cases. The Litifs received a total of $1.15 million, while the Husseys only received about $220,000. Because John McIntyre had been tortured, his family was awarded $3 million. As for the Donahues and Hallorans, they were initially awarded $6.4 million and $2 million, respectively, but an appeals panel overturned the rulings, claiming the families failed to beat the statute of limitations.

CHAPTER EIGHT

"They Got Whitey"

Olga Davis spent the last several years of her life in sorrow. To the bitter end, her mind remained as sharp as her tongue, yet her final days were clouded by the memories of death, the mysteries of injustice, and heavy doses of Valium. The medication helped her cope and function, but it didn't provide any answers as to why her life was filled with tragedy and loss. She carried the weight of that question with her until her death in 2007. She was seventy-seven years old, and she may not have known true happiness—ever.

The stress and strain of being married to an abusive husband and of giving birth to ten children would be more than most people could handle. On top of that food was always scarce. And such things as family dinners or vacations were pure folly and fantasy. If nothing else, Olga Davis was a survivor, which only added to her suffering because she outlived four of her children, and very nearly a fifth.

The death of her cruel and unusual husband may have been a blessing, but it also created a void in her life that lasted thirty-two years. She was a lonely widow with no one to console her when Ronnie was killed in prison, and his murderer was never brought to justice. Debbie disappeared six months later, and before her body was found, Sandra Davis was killed by a hit-and-run driver who was never identified. And the fourth of her ten children was buried in 2006 when Michelle died of a drug overdose. Olga was dead a year later.

She never lived to see Whitey Bulger captured or tried. And while she fought the U.S. government until she took her last breath, and she heard a judge admonish the FBI and award her family millions of dollars, she never received a penny. That victory in the courtroom may have provided some solace, but Olga's heart had been broken too many times. Her emotional scar tissue was so thickened and impenetrable that she was all out of tears when she nearly lost another one of her children. This time it was Steve.

By 2006 Steve Davis was clean and sober. He'd been to the bottom and was on his way up. The lowpoint was when his wife, Maryann, the mother of his three children, and the woman who stood by him through two stints in prison, told him to just go ahead and kill himself. "You're no good to yourself," she said. "You're no good to anyone. Go ahead then. Just do more and more until it's over."

She was referring to his heroin addiction. Steve had trouble swallowing pills, and when the cocaine he was shoving up his nose didn't produce the sought after results, he upped the ante and began snorting heroin. Steve refuses to blame his feelings of rage and helplessness after the discovery of Debbie's body, but that's what it was. "My head was so fucked up with this whole thing," is all he'll admit.

So, after a few failed attempts to get clean, including time spent in a methadone clinic, Steve was finally off drugs when he took a turn too fast and rolled his car over on an entrance ramp to I-93 just a few miles from his home. He bled profusely from gashes in his head, broke several bones, and suffered from a punctured lung. Unconscious at first, Steve remembers waking up and seeing his wife's face in a bright light. Amid the sirens and flashing lights of ambulances, fire trucks, and police cars, Steve felt only his wife's fingers gently combing through his hair. He was aware of how happy that made him. Paramedics at the scene say he died twice. They also heard him say, "I forgive you, Lord."

Rather than confessing his sins and asking forgiveness from a loving God, Steve Davis offered forgiveness to what he viewed as a vengeful God who had paired him with a terrible father, who took three sisters and one brother from him, who was nowhere to be found when he was in a heroin-induced downward spiral, and who was now about to take his wife and children away from him. His offer to forgive reflects the passing of Steve Davis's anger, at least in that moment. Steve no longer believes in God, but at the time of his near death, he says he attempted to make peace with Him.

After that, however, Steve Davis's anger grew again almost without borders. A year after his mother died, he began to understand the pain she had lived with for so many years. "I cry on a regular basis," Steve admits with his head hung so low he appears to be whispering to the table. "The pain never goes away. There's no way as a parent that ever goes away. There's just no way."

Sadly, Steve and Maryann know the anguish of losing a child. They buried their precious Debra after a fatal car accident in July 2008. Deb was twenty years old, and as beautiful as her namesake, the aunt she never met who also died far too prematurely. Steve and Maryann's daughter was drunk when she died. So was the driver of the car she was in. So, too, was another girl in the backseat—the only one to survive the single car accident.

Deb had told her parents that she was going to the Country Music Festival at Gillette Stadium in Foxboro, but she and several friends were really just going to a stadium parking lot to tailgate before the concert. They didn't have tickets. They passed the signs on Route 1 in Foxboro that read, "No ticket. No entry." And without anyone enforcing that rule, they paid forty dollars to park and pulled into Lot 11.

For the next six hours they drank. At six o'clock all non-ticket holders were told to leave. By the time Deb and two of her friends were able make their way out of the parking lot and back out to Route 1, it was nearly seven. Still smiling, but with a blood-alcohol level of .20, Deb sat in the passenger seat of a Pontiac G5, put her seatbelt on, and closed her eyes. Nineteen-year-old Alexa Latteo of Mansfield was driving with a blood-alcohol content of .24, three times the legal limit. She barely made it a mile out of the stadium when she slammed head-on into a tree. Alexa and Deb died instantly. Twenty-year-old Nina Houlihan, who was riding in the back, was taken by helicopter to Beth Israel Deaconess Medical Center for treatment of multiple fractures and a broken pelvis. She was the lone survivor.

Maryann Davis was in bed watching a movie when the news came on and reported a fatal car accident in Wrentham. The video showed a black Pontiac and the names of the deceased were not given. So, why Maryann knew immediately that her Deb was gone only a mother would know.

"You don't know anything," Steve said in an effort to calm her down. But Maryann was already sobbing uncontrollably.

She paced back and forth and found a pair of Deb's shoes in the upstairs hallway. She picked them up and held them tight to her chest.

Steve called the state police and was put on hold. "Are you kidding me?" Steve yelled to no one on the other end. "This is my daughter I'm talking about!"

Then there was the flash of blue lights outside their home followed by a knock at the door. Two hearts broke simultaneously.

"I wanted to die," Steve says.

The police officer didn't have to speak, but he did. He provided some details, but the Davises were in shock. Maryann begged the police to take her to Deb, but she was told it wouldn't be a good idea to see her. The police left, and the Davises cried. Steve wildly threw furniture against the walls. Lamps, end tables, and TV screens were broken. When he was finally exhausted, he collapsed in Maryann's arms, and they held each other until the morning. It remains the darkest day in each of their lives.

"She was an angel," Maryann said. "And she for sure is one now."

Love and pain have never been too far apart in the Davis household. Deb's pictures adorn the kitchen and several other rooms. Maryann talks to her every day. Steve drives Deb's old car around with her picture dangling from the rearview mirror. They still throw birthday parties for her and blow out the candles on her favorite cake.

"We celebrate her life," Maryann explains. "When I look at her pictures, I think of the happy memories. I cry, too, but I keep her with me all the time."

Fully acknowledging Deb's irresponsibility and her culpability in her own death, the Davises set out to stop the wild party atmosphere at the Country Music Festival. In one of her conversations with Deb's photo, Maryann said, "Deb, I promise I will do everything in my power to make sure this doesn't happen to another family."

But Steve and Maryann tried and failed to set up a meeting with Robert Kraft, owner of Gillette Stadium and the New England Patriots. They wanted him to hire more security and work with the Foxboro and State Police to enforce the "No ticket, no entry" policy. It seemed like an easy fix. The problem was that kids who sat and drank for hours were ordered off the premises and pushed out on to the roads. So, the Davises wanted the Krafts to put a stop to that. "We were about the safety," Maryann says. "We didn't want money. We wanted things to change."

And as more than one lawyer told them, the best way to get people to change is to hit them in the wallet. Thus, the Davises sued the town of Foxboro, the Kraft Group, and the stadium's private security company, Team Ops, for $10 million. "Robert Kraft could end this with a phone call," Steve Davis says. "Call me, and promise me you'll make the changes, and we'll drop the suit. It ain't about the money. I don't want his money. But I'll take it if he doesn't do the things we're asking."

The lawsuit surrounding his daughter's death was weighing heavily on Steve Davis's mind as he sat up in bed on the night of June 22, 2011. Tears had been welling up in his eyes when he got a phone call that made him smile.

"They got Whitey."

The woman on the other end of the phone was Steve's cousin, Liz McDonough. She knew the feds had arrested Bulger before the story hit the news, and before the FBI officially announced it on Twitter. She wouldn't tell Steve how she knew, but Liz McDonough was still pretty well connected. In the 1980s, she had a long-standing sexual relationship with

Mafia made man Nick Giso that produced a son. She had been a frequent visitor of the Lancaster Street garage, and regularly hung out with Bulger, Flemmi, Kaufman, and others, and she was brazen enough to challenge Flemmi on the whereabouts of Debbie Davis. "I want to know where the hell Deb is!" she had drunkenly shouted in Flemmi's face two years after Debbie had disappeared. A few months after that she was shot in the head three times. That's why she thinks Flemmi was behind that unsolved murder attempt.

"What do you mean, 'They got Whitey'?" Steve asked his cousin. "Alive?"

"Yeah, he's alive, but he ain't doing too good."

Steve hung up the phone and immediately turned on the television. He assumed there would be some sort of "Breaking News" graphic on the bottom of the screen. There wasn't. He waited for the 11:00 news to begin. Still nothing. He feverishly flipped through the channels from local to national news, but no one had the story.

"Why would she call me up just to tell me a bullshit story," Steve complained to Maryann.

But Liz had it right. The FBI had supposedly been looking for Bulger for sixteen years, but all they really needed was two days. On June 20, 2011, the FBI began running several TV spots across the country asking the public's help in finding Catherine Greig, the former dental hygienist with whom Bulger had escaped. That help arrived from long distance when the FBI tip line received a call from Reykjavik, Iceland. Anna Bjornsdottir, a former Miss Iceland 1974, was watching CNN when she saw the FBI's plea and recognized Bulger and Greig as the elderly couple she had met in Santa Monica, California.

When Bulger and Greig first went on the run, they passed quickly through New York City, Chicago, and Grand Isle,

Louisiana, but they soon settled three blocks from the Pacific Ocean on the third floor of the Princess Eugenia apartment complex in Santa Monica. It was a nice place located just three miles from the FBI headquarters in Los Angeles. They had been hiding there in plain sight since 1996, just one year after they left South Boston together. Additionally, Bulger claims he returned to Boston several times, each time heavily armed and in disguise.

Of course, Steve Davis, never trusting the FBI, wonders if they knew where Bulger was all along. He's not the only one with that suspicion, which is why FBI special agent Richard DesLauriers issued this statement denying those rumors: "Any claim that the FBI knew Mr. Bulger's whereabouts prior to the FBI's publicity efforts this week are completely unfounded. When we learned his location, he was arrested promptly."

Bjornsdottir had lived for a time at the same Princess Eugenia apartment complex as Charlie and Carol Gasko, a nice couple who she noted kept mostly to themselves. Of course, Charlie and Carol were the aliases of Bulger and Greig.

The FBI found the tip credible and immediately began surveilling the apartment building. Agents arrived early in the morning on June 22, and by six o'clock that night, they successfully lured him out of the apartment. The apartment manager called Bulger to tell him his storage locker in the garage had been broken into. Bulger came down to check it out wearing a fedora. He was immediately swarmed by FBI agents and told to get on his knees and put his hands up.

"Fuck you guys," Bulger shouted. "I'm not getting on the ground. There's grease everywhere." Bulger did get down, however, and when asked who he was, he said "Charlie Gasko."

FBI agent Scott Garriola identified himself and asked Bulger again who he was.

"You know who I am," Bulger said with more impatience than pomposity. "I'm Whitey Bulger."

They handcuffed him and brought him back upstairs. Covering the peephole, they knocked on the apartment door and told Cathy the storage locker had been broken into. She opened the door and was immediately handcuffed.

Garriola asked for permission to search the place, and Bulger obliged saying, "I'm only doing this for future considerations for Cathy." Bulger actually helped with the search. He showed them his "hides" where an arsenal of weapons were hidden. There was a hide behind a mirror in the living room, and another one behind a mirror in the bathroom. There was a shaving kit bag full of cash, fake IDs, and birth certificates for real people named James Lawlor, Ernest Beaudreau, Sidney Terry, and others. More than $820,000 was found in apartment 303.

The stash of weapons was enormous. Bulger had dozens of combat knives, and at least thirty fully functioning guns, including semi-automatics, a Baretta, three .357 Magnums, a shotgun, and hundreds of rounds of ammunition. Most of the guns were loaded.

Liz McDonough knew before the *Los Angeles Times* broke the story shortly after midnight eastern time. She knew before the FBI condensed a sixteen-year manhunt to 140 characters on Twitter: "FBI Agents in Santa Monica, CA have captured Boston Fugitive James J. 'Whitey' Bulger and his girlfriend Catherine Greig. Boston.fbi.gov" Liz McDonough knew before the Associated Press picked up the story, and before the Boston newspapers and TV stations began posting it on their websites. She had it first, and she had it right.

The news was traveling fast, but not fast enough to beat the end of the day's newscasts. Each one signed off without any word about Bulger. Steve Davis wasn't checking Twitter or the Internet, and he finally turned off his television and went to bed around 12:30 in the morning. Moments later, New England Cable News meteorologist Matt Noyes, the only on-air person still in the building, read the breaking news bulletin. By early morning, Steve woke up to an all out media blitz that could have been headlined: Liz McDonough was right!

What followed were several days of coast-to-coast activity. Bulger, looking very little like the younger version of himself on the wanted posters, smiled shamelessly for his booking photo. His full beard and mustache were neatly trimmed, and he wore a white undershirt beneath a white collared shirt. Greig was not smiling when a police officer snapped her picture.

Bulger and Greig were arraigned in a federal courtroom in downtown Los Angeles on Thursday, June 23, and then flown to Boston for a series of court appearances the following week. In his first appearance, Bulger stood before Magistrate Judge Marianne Bowler and was asked if he could afford an attorney. "Not after you took my money," he grumbled. Bulger was referring to the $822,198 dollars in cash he had stuffed in plastic bags and hidden behind the walls of his apartment, and that the FBI had seized. Agents also confiscated thirty firearms, false IDs, about a hundred handwritten pages of Bulger's memoir, copies of "America's Most Wanted" episodes that featured Bulger, closets full of unopened boxes of Q-Tips, soap and Kleenex, a stack of *Soldier of Fortune* magazines, and two holiday cards, one featuring dogs wearing Santa hats with the caption: "Merry Christmas from Santa's little yelpers."

The most excitement Bulger probably had had in years came when a motorcade brought him from the Federal Courthouse in Boston to his prison cell at the Plymouth County House of Corrections, and then again when he was flown by Coast

Guard helicopter from Plymouth back to Boston for his court appearances. An FBI agent with a machine gun was with him at all times. Motorcycle cops flanked the black SUV, not a police car, which Bulger was escorted around in. And a police boat patrolled the harbor near the court. If it weren't for the handcuffs and the orange jumpsuit he was wearing, you'd think Bulger was the president or the pope. You could tell he was enjoying his celebrity status.

Steve Davis was sickened by it. "Why the hell do they get to go in first?" Steve bellowed in court on the day Bulger's brothers, Billy and Jack, were allowed into the courtroom before the victims' families. "This won't happen again, or I'm telling you there's gonna be a big problem!"

Bulger merely mouthed the word "hello" when he passed by his brothers, and then he turned around and said "not guilty" a dozen times. His arraignment lasted about ten minutes, and he was once again flown back to his prison cell in Plymouth.

That's where he was nearly a year later when Greig reappeared in court wearing her blue two-piece prison outfit. With much less fanfare than Bulger received, Greig was driven to the John Joseph Moakley United States Courthouse in Boston in a police cruiser from the Wyatt Federal Detention Center in Rhode Island. The handcuffs behind her back were removed as she entered. She looked like she had just emerged from the shower. There was color in her cheeks and she smiled at her family sitting in the front row. She was there to be sentenced to prison after accepting a plea bargain.

The courtroom was silent, but for the tapping on several computer keyboards. There were a few whispers, but very little reaction to the sudden appearance of Whitey Bulger's girlfriend. The person who everyone in the courtroom had come to see sat in relative anonymity.

Despite a long list of persistent lies to authorities, including her claim that she didn't know about the money or the guns in her apartment, and that she didn't know about many of her own assets back in Boston, and the even more outlandish lie that she didn't have a true understanding of what Bulger was wanted for all those years, Catherine Greig was permitted to take a plea. She admitted to harboring a fugitive and identity fraud. That was it.

In her Statement of Facts filed in U.S. District Court, Greig began to reveal the entirety of her life with Whitey Bulger, but it's obvious she fell short of telling the whole truth. It's obvious there were several, perhaps many, other people involved in helping Bulger evade arrest. For instance, Greig stated that in January 1995 a "John Doe No. 1" told her that Flemmi had been arrested and that law enforcement was searching for Bulger. She doesn't identify "John Doe No. 1," but it's quite likely Kevin Weeks. Furthermore, she said, "From January 1995 through June 22, 2011, I also agreed with others, including Bulger, to harbor and conceal him from law enforcement." Later in the court filing, she said, "At various times in 1995 and 1996, Bulger arranged for me to speak with Jane Doe No. 1 and others by telephone. In order to defeat law enforcement efforts to locate him, Bulger would arrange for these calls to be received at the homes of third parties . . ."

Greig and Bulger also met with Jane and John Doe, along with a Jane Doe No. 2 at a hotel in Chicago in 1995 in order to have pictures taken for false IDs. The rest of her admissions involved the aliases she and Bulger used while traipsing from a Best Western Hotel in Holtsville, New York, to a Walmart in Louisiana to a train station in Illinois, and other stops across America. They were Mr. and Mrs. Thomas Baxter for a while, then Mark and Carol Shapeton, and finally Charles and Carol

Gasko. There were other names used at various times for which Greig only supplied initials. She and Bulger had exploited people who had problems with alcoholism or drugs, or were homeless, or had mental illnesses. For as little as $200 they could convince a desperate person to hand over their social security numbers, driver's licenses, and other forms of identification. Not only did Greig harbor a suspected serial murderer for sixteen years, she committed crimes with him along the way. And for all this, her lawyer, Kevin Reddington, was seeking a sentence of twenty-seven months. "In reference to the government's statement that she lies and lies and lies," Reddington said in court, "the truth is that when she was in California, she didn't know she had any assets. She thought it was gone."

"It's just not credible that she clean forgot," U.S. District Judge Douglas Woodlock responded.

"That's the truth, your Honor," Reddington insisted. "That's what happened."

But the judge refused to believe that Greig failed to remember she owned a mortgage-free house in Quincy and had $135,000 in a local bank account. The judge also couldn't have believed Greig knew nothing about the money hidden in the walls in Santa Monica. Neither Greig nor Bulger had had a job for sixteen years, yet he provided her with money to pay their rent in cash, and for all their groceries, and other expenses. Where did she think that money was coming from? Plus, she admitted that Bulger had told her that if he died first, she had two options: to remain in Santa Monica alone or go home. And of course the only way she could do either is if she had access to and control of the cash. Still, the tale Reddington spun was a love story.

"Catherine Greig fell in love with Mr. Bulger," Reddington said. "And that's why she was in the situation she was in. . . .

You look at this woman at the age of sixty who was living with a man whom she truly loved. She took him to the dentist. She cooked for him. She was basically his housemaid. Her life consisted of living in that apartment, shopping for him, rescuing animals and going for walks. She has accepted responsibility. Judge, you are to impose a fair sentence, not a vengeful one."

Steve Davis and the other victims' family members sat in the courtroom listening attentively and watching Greig's every move. For the first forty-five minutes, she barely moved. She sat with a nearly rigid posture with only a slight curve in her shoulders brought on by age. She didn't reposition herself in her chair, and she didn't talk to her lawyer. She also didn't show any emotion until the families delivered their impact statements. Steve Davis made her cringe. Timmy Connors got her to cry.

Connors was still an infant when his father, Eddie, was killed by Bulger on June 12, 1975. The day of the Greig sentencing was Timmy's thirty-seventh birthday. "You're not here by choice," he began, speaking directly to Greig. "You're only here because you were caught. You're a cold-hearted criminal who never showed any sympathy to any of us. The only emotion you ever showed is when your brother was mentioned. Truth be told, if I had a sister like you, I would have killed myself, too."

There was an audible gasp in the courtroom. Greig put her hands to her face and began to cry. It took several minutes for her to regain her composure. Connors threw that emotional haymaker and it landed. Was Greig remembering the suicide, or was she wondering if she had just spent sixteen years with the man who killed her brother?

Back in 1972, then twenty-year-old Catherine Greig had married Bobby McGonagle. Within two years, Bulger had allegedly killed Bobby's twin brothers, Donnie and Paul

McGonagle. And before he died of a drug overdose in 1987, Bobby had told Catherine many times that he knew Bulger was guilty of killing his brothers. Why would Greig have run off with the man who killed two of her brothers-in-law? Stranger still is that Greig's brother, David, was a close associate of Bulger's up until the fateful day in 1984 that he was found shot to death in a home on Cape Cod. The shooting was ruled a suicide, though many suspect David Greig tried to blackmail Bulger regarding their alleged homosexual relationship.

"Judge, I ask you," Connors continued. "If you give a sentence any less than what the government is asking, you may as well stick this pen in my eye, because you'd be causing me that much pain."

Paul McGonagle, Jr., whose father had been married to Greig's twin sister Margaret, also delivered an impact statement. "Catherine Greig betrayed our family," he said. "This woman provided invaluable assistance to Bulger. The last time I saw my father he was with my brother to get ice cream. I never saw him again. Twenty-seven years went by before I knew his fate. My father was a great father," Paul continued. "No matter his faults, he did not deserve to die the way he did."

The last of the victims' family members to speak was Steve Davis. Reddington knew Steve was a loose canon and his unpredictability worried him. He tried to preempt Steve's influence by filing a motion with the court suggesting Steve's frequent media interviews could unfairly affect the impartiality of the sentencing. Here is an excerpt from Reddington's written statement:

> The United States Attorney was then subjected to a firestorm of media hype based upon the criticism leveled by the "victims," spearheaded by the ubiquitous Steven Davis. It was

then and only then that a full court press was organized to bury Catherine Greig with a severe prison sentence coupled by a demand for exorbitant fines and seizure of everything she owns. The apparent self-anointed spokesman for "the victims" is Mr. Davis. The ever garrulous Davis and his incessant press conferences and criticism of the United States Attorney's Offices as well as the "evil" Greig is clearly the "tail waggin' the dog." He criticizes and denigrates the U.S Attorney when he does not agree with their direction in the resolution of the case. He is in constant contact with the media reveling in his press conferences in front of the courthouse. He has been interviewed and made numerous comments about his plans to go to California for consultation regarding his "movie" as well as his book that he is writing. . . . He noted that he wanted Ms. Greig to serve at least sixteen years, but "ten would do."

Steve Davis approached the microphone located in the public seating area of the courtroom wearing a tan suit over a stylish T-shirt. His brown Ray-Ban sunglasses hung on the collar, and the notes he had been fumbling with since the start of the proceedings were crumpled up in his pocket. The impact statement he prepared would not be the one he delivered. That first version said, in part, "In all fairness, Catherine Greig was not directly involved in any of these murders. However, she did everything in her power to ensure that these victims' families never saw justice done. Her sympathies lay with Bulger, the murderer, rather than with his victims. She had not one bit of concern or sympathy for these victims or their families. Any request for leniency should be measured against her lack of sympathy for the murdered victims."

But that statement had gone through many last minute revisions. Yellow and blue hi-liter marks covered the pages.

Steve even had a friend re-write the statement for him, but when he read it, it didn't sound like him. So, as he stepped nervously up to the mike, he was determined to speak from the heart. He paused and briefly surveyed the courtroom. Then, after a short, but deep breath, he plucked the crumpled piece of paper out of his pocket, and began to read.

"I'm speaking on behalf of my mother, and my sister, Debra Davis," he said with an uncharacteristically soft tone. "Since my sister's disappearance in 1981 until my mother died, she never stopped grieving." Steve knew his statement was without its intended impact. His reading of it was monotone and stiff. This was an important moment for him, one that he waited many years for, and he was blowing it. So, he stopped reading and he looked directly at Greig. She was a mere twenty feet away from him with her back turned. "This woman does not deserve any leniency at all!" he said forcefully. "She should get the maximum! She doesn't even have the heart to look any of us in the eye!" His anger was growing, so he paused again to try to calm himself down. He failed. "Catherine, you're a dirty bitch! Thank you, your Honor."

With that, Steve shuffled back to his seat. The reaction in the courtroom was an odd mix of disdain and understanding. On one side of the courtroom sat Catherine Greig, an elderly woman who slept with and harbored a man who killed his way to the top and ratted on his friends. She helped Bulger run like a coward and she repeated his lies every day for sixteen years. She loved a man who should have been unlovable, yet she received an unexpected level of sympathy when Steve Davis, the long-suffering brother of one of Bulger's victims was mean to her. Even the judge thought Steve had overstepped the boundaries of decent behavior. Speaking directly to Greig, he said, "I gave a lot of thought about the presentation from the victims. It was cruel, crude, and heartfelt, reflecting vengeance and wanting to get back. I didn't like the way Mr. Davis spoke to you, but there is a hard lesson from the acts of cruelty toward you. It's that we're all responsible for what we do."

With that summary remark, Judge Woodlock was ready to issue Greig's sentence. In the short pause that followed, Steve's mind raced. Like a man falling to his death, his life flashed before his eyes. He saw the graves of his father, and brother, and two of his sisters. He felt his mother's tears, and recalled his wife's uncontrollable sobs when his daughter died. His life was pretty good, but too often unfair. He fought the moment of self-pity where he anticipated the judge pronouncing a punishment that didn't even come close to fitting the crime. He wasn't sure he could handle that. He saw the younger face of Whitey Bulger, the one that threatened him at Triple O's so many years ago, and he associated his rage for Bulger with the woman waiting now to learn her fate.

"Don't feel bad for her because she's sixty-one," Davis wanted to tell the judge. "She knew what she was getting into. She was trash on the street in South Boston when she was a teenager. She's no different now. She's just an older woman. You sleep with the devil, you gotta pay!" Steve was so deep in thought, he almost missed it when the judge gave Catherine Greig ninety-six months in prison and a $150,000 fine.

"Nice," Steve said as he did the quick math in his head. Later he told reporters, "We'll never be satisfied. The judge gave her what he thought was fair, and we have to accept that. She got an eight-year sentence. All the victims' families served a life sentence."

Greig would spend the next eight years of her life in the Federal Correctional Institution in Waseca, Minnesota, located some seventy-five miles south of Minneapolis. It was a low security facility for female inmates. It was the first morsel of justice for Steve Davis and the other victims' families. But the person they really wanted was Bulger.

"I'd hang Whitey as quick as look at him," Davis thought. "He likes Southie so much, I'd chain him to the back of my car and drag him through South Boston. The guy who goes out and murders nineteen people, whether he's fifteen or a hundred and fifteen, he's still a creep murderer. This isn't closure. It's only a beginning. The full justice will be when Bulger's gone."

The trial of James "Whitey" Bulger's was originally scheduled for November 2012. It was postponed until March and then June 2013. Along the way, Bulger took at least three suspicious trips to Boston for alleged health issues that included an irregular heartbeat. Steve Davis speculated that Bulger was still receiving special considerations and that Bulger's hospital visits were nothing more than opportunities to meet with his brothers. His attorney, J. W. Carney, indicated that the long days in solitary confinement were taking a toll on Bulger, and there were conflicting reports that suggested Bulger was either in great physical condition and doing a hundred push-ups a day, or he was in failing health and wearing adult diapers.

Finally, two years after his arrest, Bulger would stand trial. The legal wrangling and maneuvering was over. Bulger's biggest defeat before the trial began was the ruling that he would not be allowed to use the bogus defense that former federal prosecutor Jeremiah O'Sullivan had given him immunity. Bulger claimed that O'Sullivan had made him a verbal promise in 1984 that exonerated him from all prior and future crimes "up to and including murder." There had been nothing in writing, and O'Sullivan didn't have the authority to make such a promise anyway, but Bulger still made the ridiculous claim that only served to reveal a glaring contradiction in his pre-trial defense.

On the one hand, he claimed he wasn't an informant, and on the other hand, he claimed he had immunity. So, the obvious unanswered question is why would he be granted immunity if he hadn't been helping law enforcement?

O'Sullivan denied protecting Bulger from prosecution for violent crimes when he testified under oath before Congress in 2002, and he died in 2009. So, it was Bulger's word against the sworn testimony of a dead man, and the presiding judge chose the dead man's. Bulger's ace in the hole was ripped from his hands. That decision was handed down on May 1. The trial would begin five weeks later.

In between, Steve Davis punched a guy at Starbucks. The incident probably reveals the level of stress Steve was under at the time. He was anxious about being called to testify in the Bulger trial, and his lawsuit involving his daughter's death was constantly on his mind. But the right cross he threw at a Milton coffee shop was also an indicator of how little Steve Davis trusts law enforcement to this day.

Steve's wife, Maryann, was hiding out in a Starbucks bathroom stall when she called Steve to say a strange man was following her. She had noticed him watching her at two previous stops, and when he showed up at Starbucks, she got scared.

"Get out of the bathroom," Steve directed. "Get out in the open around people. I'll be right there." Steve sped through the town of Milton not knowing what to think. He worried that the guy could be a sexual predator, maybe a mugger, or even one of Steve's enemies. He still had some of those. Despite being an agnostic, he asked God to keep Maryann safe. When Steve got to Starbucks, he spotted Maryann who nodded in the direction of a younger man in his mid-thirties standing in line. Steve moved slowly, looking this way and that, until he quite casually made his way over to the stranger. He paused briefly, and looked back at Maryann to confirm that this was the guy. It was. Steve put his hand on the man's shoulder, leaned in close to his ear and said, "What the fuck you following my wife for?"

Startled, the man looked first at Steve, whose eyes were wide and lips were tight, and then the man made the mistake of looking over at Maryann. That was his tell. "I don't even know her," the man said meekly.

Steve then popped him in the mouth. It was a quick burst of anger thrown forcefully with a rotating shoulder and a clenched fist. The man fell backward into a display stand of coffee mugs and CDs. He stumbled but didn't fall. Steve stood in a fighter's stance and watched as the man struggled to regain his balance. A stunned group of patrons and baristas stared in disbelief. Suddenly, the man made a dash for the back door with Steve in hot pursuit. The chase ended quickly with Steve standing on a busy street corner watching the man with the bloody lip racing down the street. Maryann came out and joined him. She slid up next to him, held his hand, and whispered "thank you" in his ear. Steve went back into Starbucks, apologized for the mess, and got a coffee to go.

The Davises didn't know who the strange man was until the Milton police showed up at their door later that day. The officer explained that the man was an insurance investigator assigned to follow Maryann, who had recently filed a workman's compensation claim. If he had simply identified himself, Steve said, he might not have gotten a fat lip. The man was pressing charges. So, there would be yet another court appearance for Steve Davis. Meanwhile, he spent every day of the summer of 2013 in a courtroom with Whitey Bulger. And every day, he fought the impulse to fire off another right cross at the man he believes killed his sister.

The building that once housed Triple O's (left) now finds itself across the street from a Starbucks in a gentrified South Boston.
(PHOTO CREDIT: ASSOCIATED PRESS)

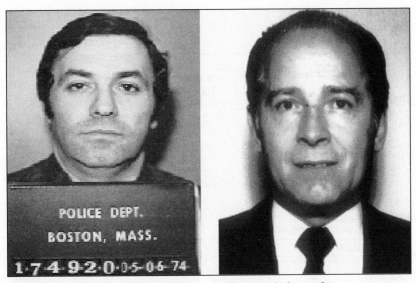

Mugshots of Stephen "The Rifleman" Flemmi (left) and James "Whitey" Bulger (right) taken in 1983, almost two years after Debbie Davis went missing.
(PHOTO CREDIT: ASSOCIATED PRESS)

The FBI considered Bulger one of their best informants, which is why they included "TE" (top echelon) on his informant card. Bulger and Flemmi's informant cards were presented as evidence during Bulger's 2013 federal trial.

Flemmi's FBI informant card listed him as a real estate agent. His file was "closed" in 1982.

A wedding photo of the Davis family. Debbie and Steve Davis are on the far right.
(COURTESY OF STEVE DAVIS)

A personal snapshot of Stephen Flemmi and Debbie Davis when they were dating.
(COURTESY OF STEVE DAVIS)

A photo of Debbie Davis in the early 1980s. Her sister Eileen would later say, "I couldn't see Flemmi killing her, because she was his trophy."
(COURTESY OF STEVE DAVIS)

An undated surveillance photo of Stephen Flemmi originally released by the FBI.
(PHOTO CREDIT: ASSOCIATED PRESS)

An undated surveillance photo that shows James "Whitey" Bulger (left) with his former bodyguard and fellow gang member, Kevin Weeks. At Bulger's trial, Weeks shouted from the witness stand, "I've been lying all my life. I'm a criminal!"
(PHOTO CREDIT: ASSOCIATED PRESS)

FBI Special Agent John Connolly leaving federal court after being found guilty. He was sentenced to forty years in prison for slipping information to Bulger and Flemmi.
(PHOTO CREDIT: ASSOCIATED PRESS)

Former FBI supervisor John Morris testifying at John Connolly's trial. During the 2013 trial of James "Whitey" Bulger, Morris apologized to the victims' families, saying, "I don't ask for your forgiveness, but I do want to express my sincere apology for things I may have done and for things I didn't do."
(PHOTO CREDIT: ASSOCIATED PRESS)

Court drawing of Steve Davis (far right) disrupting court while Stephen Flemmi was on the witness stand.
(Photo credit: Associated Press)

Courtroom sketch of Stephen Flemmi testifying in the 2013 trial of Whitey Bulger. He and Bulger had not seen each other in almost two decades.
(Photo credit: Associated Press)

Steve Davis talking to reporters outside the courthouse.

Steve Davis holding a photo of his sister, Debbie.

CHAPTER NINE

The Trial Starts

When Whitey Bulger awoke at the Plymouth County House of Corrections on the morning of June 12, 2013, it was still dark outside, though his windowless cell offered no evidence of that. Opting for a casual look on the first day of his trial, Bulger put on a pair of blue jeans and a green long sleeved shirt. The handcuffs placed on his wrists were an unwanted accessory, but they would be removed before he entered court and heard Assistant U.S. Attorney Brian Kelly tell a jury what this trial was all about. "It's about a criminal enterprise that ran amock in Boston for thirty years," Kelly began, "and at the center of it all is one man, James Bulger. He started out as just one of many in this enterprise, and he eventually took control. And he did the dirty work himself, because he is a hands-on killer."

Bulger had no reaction to the accusation, but Steve Davis, who was sitting right behind him, smiled just a little. This was not a happy occasion, and the upward turn on Davis's lips did not reflect a happy smile. The truth appeared in Davis's eyes, which were still somewhat reddened by his sadly nostalgic drive into court that morning.

The expressway had been jammed up with commuter traffic, so Steve decided to use the back roads. That meant taking a right on Hallett Street and passing Florian Hall in Dorchester. Steve sat a traffic light and remembered how cold it was the day authorities found the bodies of Deborah Hussey, Bucky Barrett, and John McIntyre behind the building. And there was very nearly a fourth victim. The night Weeks, Flemmi, and Bulger buried the bodies there, a young man drove into the parking lot to relieve himself. Weeks testified that he stopped digging and waited quietly out of sight. When the man drove off, Bulger said, "You should have shot him. There's plenty of room in the hole."

After a right at the lights, Steve was soon upon the entrance to Tenean Beach where Paul McGonagle had been buried. Whenever the tide ebbed and flowed over McGonagle's shallow grave, Weeks said Bulger liked to joke, "Drink up, Paulie."

Less than a mile up the road, Steve glanced to his right and saw the beginning of the Neponset River Bridge where he spent weeks hoping they'd find his sister's body, while simultaneously hoping they wouldn't.

He merged on to Morrissey Boulevard and passed the section of that road where John Martorano killed Billy O'Brien by mistake. Martorano was targeting a criminal named Ralph DiMasi, but the hail of gunfire only wounded DiMasi eight times, and killed O'Brien who was out buying a birthday cake for his twelve-year-old daughter. O'Brien had only met DiMasi a few hours earlier, and was simply giving this friend of his ex-wife a ride.

Further up Morrissey Boulevard is where Bulger and Flemmi killed Eddie Connors. The phone booth where his body was found riddled with machine gun bullets is no longer there, but the fondness of that memory still remains with Bulger. Eight months before his trial began, Bulger talked to his nephew, Billy, on the phone from prison. He was recorded making a machine gun sound while reminiscing about the murder of Eddie Connors.

Steve shook his head and continued along this road map of human tragedy. At the end of Morrissey Boulevard is a rotary with exits for William J. Day Boulevard and Old Colony Boulevard. Old Colony is where Rotary Liquors was located, and where Bulger and Flemmi regularly extorted money from bookies and drug dealers. Anthony Attardo was one such coke dealer who initially refused to pay the money Bulger demanded from him. "I tried not to pay him," Attardo testified. "He said, 'I want $100,000, or something's gonna happen.' I thought something was gonna happen to me. My brother ended up being shot. He was seventeen at the time."

The day after seventeen-year-old Tommy Attardo was shot, Bulger told Anthony, "You're next. Now give me my money!"

Anthony brought all the money he could get his hands on down to Rotary Liquors. It was only $80,000, but Bulger told him not to worry about the rest.

"Why did you decide to pay Mr. Bulger?" Attardo was asked in court.

"Because I got four other brothers and five sisters," he replied. "I thought it was best just to pay him."

Steve Davis veered right on to William J. Day Boulevard. Carson Beach was now on his right. That's where Tommy King was picked up before being shot in the head and disposed of not far from Steve's sister.

A left on to L Street meant Steve would cross over East Broadway where Triple O's used to be. This is the route he took when he met Bulger at Triple O's some thirty years ago.

The next crossroad was East Third Street, and Steve couldn't help but glance in the direction of the home where his sister was killed.

Steve knew this section of South Boston very well, and managed to avoid all the significant traffic along the way to the courthouse. The last part of the trip put him on Seaport Boulevard where Brian Halloran and Michael Donahue were gunned down by Bulger and, the evidence suggests, Pat Nee. Steve was stopped at a light outside the bar, The Whisky Priest, thinking that this was very nearly the exact spot where Donahue's car had rolled to a stop.

Finally, Steve's journey that covered eight miles and forty years brought him to the John J. Moakley Courthouse, the site where Flemmi committed his first murder when he gunned down Punchy McLaughlin.

Minutes later, Steve was sitting in the courtroom waiting for Bulger's trial to begin. It didn't take long for him to start wondering why there needed to be a trial at all after Bulger's defense attorney, J. W. Carney, admitted to no fewer than twenty-three felony counts in his opening statements. Carney seemed to be bragging about it. "What the evidence will show is that Jim Bulger is a person who had an unbelievably lucrative criminal enterprise in Boston," Carney said in his unconventional defense. "He was making millions and millions of dollars. He had law enforcement on his payroll. I tell you this history so that you will understand the depth of corruption that existed among law enforcement during this period. It puts in context what happens after 1994. This was how James Bulger was able to do illegal gambling, make illegal loans, engage in drug trafficking, and extortion, and never ever be charged, and on top of that make millions upon millions upon millions of dollars doing so."

Carney, a former prosecutor, is considered brilliant by his peers. He's defended people like John C. Salvi, III, who killed two people when he shot up two abortion clinics in Brookline, and James Keown, who was accused of poisoning his wife with antifreeze.

Carney began his defense by acknowledging that Bulger was guilty of nearly everything he was charged with. With eleven members of the jury listening intently and one dozing off, Carney claimed "the height of Jim Bulger's criminal activities" was 1982 to 1990. He then laid out an excellent case for the prosecution. "Jim Bulger was involved in illegal gaming, football cards. It's called in the business—bookmaking," Carney clearly explained to the jury. "He also loaned money to people at extremely high rates. That's called loansharking. He also was involved in drug dealing. These crimes, that's what he did. And in order to protect this business, he paid corrupt law enforcement officials."

The entire courtroom, except for Bulger, nodded in agreement. Bulger sat stoically, though at times he would feverishly write on a yellow legal pad. He showed no emotion, never smiled, and seemed undisturbed by his lawyer's surprisingly honest approach. Clearly, Bulger had no delusions that he would ever spend another day as a free man. If there were twelve people in the world who didn't already know that Bulger was guilty, they were sitting on the jury, and they knew it now. Carney made sure of that, and then he made sure to tell everyone what this trial was really all about. "James Bulger never ever was an informant for John Connolly," Carney stated authoritatively. He paused to let the declarative statement linger. He knew he had hit on an issue of great fascination. Never mind that Bulger wasn't charged with being an informant, nor is it a crime to be one, Bulger's one hope for this trial was that he could convince the world that he wasn't a rat. Carney held the courtroom's attention, but he was about to lose his credibility. He gave two reasons he believed offered proof that Bulger was not an informant. "Number one," he began, "James Bulger is of Irish descent. And the worst thing an Irishman could do is to become an informant." Stifled laughter was heard throughout the courtroom. "The second reason is a practical one," Carney continued. "He was not deeply tied to the Italian mafia."

Carney was suggesting that Bulger wasn't an informant because he didn't have any information to give law enforcement, yet Carney had already admitted that Bulger was deeply involved in organized crime. So, of course, he had knowledge that could help law enforcement. He didn't need to be tied in with the Mafia to offer up information.

Carney then turned his focus on FBI agent John Connolly. He accused Connolly of creating an informant file for Bulger and then stuffing it with some seven hundred pages of information that was either fabricated or had come from other sources. According to Carney, Connolly wanted his FBI associates to believe Bulger was an informant, so he could keep Bulger out of jail, and Bulger's informant status would explain why he was meeting with Bulger on a regular basis. Carney still had to explain *why* Bulger met with Connolly. "If he [Bulger] ever was going to be indicted," Carney explained, "he wanted a heads up so he could leave town. That's what he was paying for."

Bulger may indeed have gotten his money's worth when the indictments against him came down in 1995, and he was alerted by John Connolly that it was time to leave town. Connolly had trouble finding Bulger at first, so he called Kevin O'Neil at Triple O's and told him to get a message to "the kid," Kevin Weeks. "Tell him his friend has a problem," Connolly told O'Neil in a cryptically coded, but abundantly clear directive. O'Neil testified he never delivered the message though, because later that same day, he saw Connolly walking out of the South Boston Liquor Mart with Weeks.

Carney told the jury a different version of these events. He declared that Bulger had heard about the indictments on a radio report when he was driving back from vacation, so he simply "turned around and drove elsewhere. That's why he was not arrested," Carney continued. "It was something as mundane as that."

However he heard the news, Bulger initially picked up his girlfriend, Theresa Stanley, and later returned to Boston to trade her in for Catherine Greig. Only then did he drive elsewhere and, according to Carney, Bulger "settled in California. Not hiding. Living openly in plain sight while those FBI agents pretended to look for him."

Carney's strategy started to crystallize as he moved toward the conclusion of his opening statement. His efforts during this trial, he said, would be to show that the government was corrupt, that Bulger was not an FBI informant, that he did not kill Debbie Davis or Deborah Hussey, and that the key witnesses who would testify against Bulger were all liars who had received reduced sentences and other benefits from the government to tell their lies.

One of these alleged "liars" was Winter Hill Gang member John Martorano. "John Martorano is one of the scariest psychopaths in Boston history," Carney stated. "He would kill people almost randomly. He would kill people because they crossed him. He would kill people because he wanted to get their money. He would kill people as easily as we would order a cup of coffee."

Martorano has testified before and would testify in this trial, that some of his killings were with and for Whitey Bulger.

"The evidence related to John Martorano's state of mind will be the key to accepting whether he is a credible witness," Carney continued. "John Martorano knew how this process worked. He knew how a gangster could make a deal with the federal government and get an extraordinary benefit if he testified against the people they wanted to prosecute."

Carney made eye contact with the members of the jury, trying to read their faces. He seemed to be looking for some kind of engagement so he could believe he at least had a fighting chance. When he told the jury that Martorano had pled guilty to committing twenty murders, but served only twelve years in prison, he may have wanted to see shock and outrage. "The Federal government was so desperate to have John Martorano testify against John Connolly and James Bulger," Carney said, "they basically put their hands in the air and said take anything you want."

Martorano called the shots, Carney explained. He didn't want to be prosecuted in the death penalty states of Oklahoma and Florida for the Wheeler and Callahan murders, and he wasn't. He didn't want to testify against his brother, and he wasn't required to. He wanted to keep some of his property, and that was permitted. He also received $250,000 for the movie rights to his life. Carney was implying that this psychopathic killer was not only a free man, but a rich one, and that it was all courtesy of the federal government.

"Ask yourself," Carney addressed the jury, "would John Martorano be willing to lie about James Bulger?" Perhaps Carney had persuaded at least some of the members of the jury that the answer was yes. Now, it was time for Carney to discredit Kevin Weeks and Stephen Flemmi. Weeks had spent nearly every day with Bulger for about thirteen years, and he and Flemmi probably knew Bulger better than anyone. Their testimony would be critical to the prosecution. Their credibility had to be impeached if the defense was to succeed.

"Kevin Weeks admitted to killing five people," Carney informed the jury before taking the same tack he did with Martorano. "Prosecutors gave him a total of five years. He got to keep his movie and book rights. I submit Kevin Weeks can't tell the truth even when there is nothing at stake for him."

Next, Carney turned the spotlight on Flemmi, who was one half of the two-headed monster that had terrorized South Boston for twenty years. Like Martorano, he was also facing the death penalty in Oklahoma and Florida. He also was allowed to keep some of his property and bank accounts, but his deal with the government wasn't quite as good, Carney explained, because "he was the third person through the door." Martorano and Weeks had already cut their deals, so Flemmi's cooperation had less value. Still, for life imprisonment rather than execution, Flemmi would have been willing to lie about his long-time friend and partner who he thought was gone forever. "At this point," Carney argued, "So many years had gone by that it's fair to say Flemmi thought he'd never see Bulger again. So, he decided to start blaming Jim Bulger for crimes he himself had carried out."

Carney backed up this contention by giving four examples. He told the jury of the Wheeler and Callahan murders pointing out that Bulger wasn't there for either one. He explained who Deborah Hussey was and said Bulger had no motive to kill her, but Steve Flemmi did. And Carney suggested the same reasoning regarding the murder of Debbie Davis. "She was Flemmi's girlfriend for years," Carney said. "He was extremely generous to her and her family. He was very proud to have her as a girlfriend. But he learned she was cheating on him. He learned that she was mocking him as an old man, and that she was going to continue to take his money. And when you're dating a psychopathic killer, that's the last thing you want him to know."

Steve Davis sat there with his pulse rising. He had tried to prepare himself for what was guaranteed to be an emotional few months. He knew he'd hear things about his sister's death that would bring back a lot of his pain. He anticipated seeing photos of Debbie smiling happily in life, and other photos of her decayed bones and skull after her body was exhumed. He expected some days to be more difficult than others, but he never imagined his sister would be described in unflattering terms.

"I didn't like how he was painting my sister almost like a dirty tramp, and a cheat," Davis complained after court. "My sister wasn't like that. He didn't know about their relationship. He had no right saying that, because he didn't know her. She was a sweetheart. Don't paint her as some kind of street tramp."

Davis was also surprised when he heard Carney inform the jury that Flemmi once told Martorano that he was the one who strangled Debbie Davis. Steve Davis didn't believe it, but he had to reconsider when Martorano testified to it during the trial. "None of his opening lying made any sense to me," Davis said of Carney. "If he's that smart of a lawyer, he knows there's no winning this case. He's gonna lose. He's gonna have to swallow it."

As Carney said to the *Boston Globe* on July 1, 2011, "This is the latest case I have where I have a client who is in a jam, and I'm going to be the person to try to get him out." Applied to Bulger, his use of the term "jam" may be the understatement of the century. Undoubtedly, Carney knew he had a loser of a client and a loser of a case, but in putting on a defense to the best of his ability, he took the only option available to him. He needed to impeach the likes of John Martorano, Kevin Weeks, and Steve Flemmi, in hopes of leaving the jury confused about the real truth. That's the only chance he had to put reasonable doubt into the minds of the jurors.

"Given these three individuals," Carney said. "Given their background, given their character, if that was all you knew, would you believe them? I suggest it is an unreliable recipe to get the truth."

There couldn't have been too many people in the courtroom or in the public who expected the Bulger trial to reveal the absolute truth. After all, the so-called facts were all being supplied by a bunch of bookies, drug dealers, and other criminals prone to extortion and murder—all of them with something to hide and motives to lie. Any truth was likely to come out by accident and remain shrouded in hyperbole, legend, and self-delusion.

"I'm not gonna get the truth, not one hundred percent," Steve Davis lamented as he drove back home on the same path of destruction on which his day started. "They're all full of shit. It's the justice system."

Steve stopped at the intersection of East Third Street. Horns blared behind him, but he stubbornly kept his foot on the brake of his deceased daughter's car. He looked at his young Deb's picture, the one he kept taped to the dashboard. He knew the truth about her death, but did he really know what happened to his sister? Oblivious to the growing impatience of drivers around him, Steve looked up East Third and realized he couldn't even know for sure that Debbie was killed on this street, or in the house that Flemmi claimed the murder occurred. There's no evidence, he thought, only the word of Flemmi—a notorious liar. All Steve could do was put the pieces together himself, and hope to stumble upon a truth he could be satisfied with. But he was suddenly frightened. What if the jury had the same doubts he had?

"It's gonna be one fucking day in court if it goes any other way," he said referring to the verdict concerning Debbie's murder. "I know they'll be pulling me out of there if they ever come out with a 'not guilty.' They better hope I don't lunge too quick, because he's gonna pay for it. I do believe he did it. I do believe that Flemmi lied all his life, but that was the truth what he said. The bodies were buried where Bulger wanted them buried. He's associated with it. I'm expecting a guilty."

Steve's rationale for putting the murder on Bulger is that it all boils down to the proximity to Billy Bulger's house. "Steve Flemmi's mother lived right across the street from Billy Bulger," Davis explains. "I know if I'm sitting in my living room or kitchen, I know what's going on outside. If you look at Flemmi's house, there's motion sensors. Paranoid as they are, they're watching next door. They know what's going on. They were so close they could hear a door open, or people walking in. They had to see something. Three people go in, and two come out with a bag. Being a former criminal myself, if my brother was a politician who lived next door, you better ask me for permission to do anything in that house, because if anything came down, it would be an embarrassment to him. And Whitey probably wanted to be a part of it anyway. He didn't like my sister. And she didn't like him."

Steve's firm belief is that it was Flemmi's idea to kill Debbie, not Bulger's. Flemmi, he said, couldn't accept the fact that Debbie was leaving him, so he wanted to kill her. Steve didn't believe Flemmi's explanation that Bulger initiated the idea of killing Debbie when he discovered she knew about his relationship with John Connolly. "It was Flemmi's idea," Steve Davis stated assertively, "and his idea to ask Whitey's help with doing it. In that situation, Steve feared Whitey, and he would have needed permission, because the body's gotta come out of that house. I believe Steve couldn't look at her and pull it off. He didn't want to shoot her. This is what I believe. I don't think he had the heart to do it. After the fact, when Whitey killed her, he had the heart to pull her teeth out and cut her hands off. I believe that, because now he's gotta clean up a mess that he created. It was like, 'You do this part of it. I'll do that part of it.' Because I don't believe Steve could have done that part."

Steve sounded convincing, until it became evident that he hadn't even convinced himself. "But they're all fucking liars," he blurted out in a moment of frustration while slamming his foot down on the accelerator, finally leaving the East Third intersection. The car moved rapidly, but time passed slowly before Steve finally spoke again. With less traffic in the afternoon, he decided to take the Expressway home. To his left, he could see over the water to the edge of South Boston. Further up on his right was the Neponset River Bridge—out of sight, but not out of mind.

"All we can do is let the jury decide this in the end. It'll be in their hands. Put it this way, we know one of them did it."

CHAPTER TEN

A Confederacy of Liars

A front row seat to the Whitey Bulger trial was a precious thing. Large crowds of people lined up outside the courtroom early each morning as if they were waiting to purchase concert tickets or the latest product made by Apple. These people were gripped by a fascination with the violent tales of South Boston's yesteryear. They were there to see Whitey Bulger, and to hear the evidence against him. What they saw and heard was an assortment of bookies, loansharks, drug dealers, thieves, and murderers. Each one was a character right out of central casting. Some of them were even likable. All of them were liars. The only absolute truth promulgated from the Bulger trial came from the victim's families, forensic scientists, and at least for this case, the few honest police officers.

"My father always taught me never to trust a cop," Steve Davis said on his way to court one morning. "It's like a snake. He can be your friend, but some day he might bite you." Steve sat in court each day trying to sift through the lies like a gold

miner with a sluice box. He didn't trust the cops or the criminals, but he was able to extract a few nuggets from the best and
the worst of the thugs called to testify. Some of what they said
was probably true. Most of what they said, even if it was only
partially true, was particularly damning to Bulger. Other dec-
larations simply rang true, because they sounded so familiar.

"The room was like a hall with large windows," Steve heard
Michael Solimando say from the witness stand. Solimando was
describing his encounter with Bulger at Triple O's. "It looked
like it could be an auditorium," Solimando continued. "They
had the shades pulled down, and the only light coming in was
coming through the shades. It was not a comfortable place."

Steve could relate. He'd been in that same room on the
second floor of Triple O's and shared the same recollections of
fear and helplessness.

Like Steve, Solimando voluntarily put himself in Bulger's
zone of danger. He wasn't asking for trouble, but the choices
that led him to Triple O's were suspect. He was a self-employed
contractor who liked to hang out at Jimmy Martorano's restaurant, Chandler's. He even played for Chandler's softball
team. He was the shortstop. Brian Halloran was the first
baseman.

Eventually Jimmy Martorano introduced Solimando to
Steve Flemmi, pointing out that the two fitness buffs were
also neighbors in Milton. With those things in common,
Solimando and Flemmi began going on five mile runs together
a few times a week. Over time, Solimando met John Connolly,
and also became close friends with John Callahan. In February
1982, Solimando and Callahan bought the property at 126
High Street in Boston. Solimando's brother-in-law, Gene Kelly,
went in on the deal as an equal partner. All three men invested
$150,000 each.

By July Callahan confided in Solimando that he knew for a fact that Brian Halloran had been killed because he was working with law enforcement. Then Callahan said, "Whitey and Stevie don't think I'll stand up." Solimando pressed him on what that meant, but Callahan told him to forget it. Solimando may have been able to do just that, but the memory of their conversation came rushing back to him when he heard his friend had been killed.

Not long after Callahan's murder, Solimando was summoned to Triple O's. When he got there, Flemmi greeted him cordially. Kevin Weeks came in wearing a green Boston Celtics jacket, and Bulger waited upstairs. When Solimando got to the top of the stairs at Triple O's, he saw Bulger sitting at a card table. Bulger stood up and shook Solimando's hand, and the two men sat down to conduct business. "Mr. Bulger took a revolver out and stuck it in my face," Solimando testified. "He said, 'We want our money,' and I kept telling him I didn't know what he was talking about."

Bulger either believed or lied that Callahan owed him and Flemmi a lot of money, and that Callahan had said the money was in the building at 126 High Street.

"It can't be in the building," Solimando protested. "I don't know anything about this."

"This is only business," Flemmi said to his running partner. "We just want our money back."

Solimando had the presence of mind to ask Bulger to take the gun out of his face, but his request was not granted. Instead, Weeks handed Bulger a machine gun. Bulger placed it on his lap under the table and kept it pointed at Solimando's groin.

"Four hundred thousand dollars," Bulger said. "And if you think you're gonna go to law enforcement, we're gonna know the minute you walk on the twelfth floor of the federal building. Forget about the Boston Police Department. We're gonna know. So, get the money. We don't care where you get it." Bulger told Solimando that he knew where his sister and brother-in-law lived, and that if Solimando didn't come up with the money, somebody was going to get killed. "When we killed Halloran," Bulger admitted with a smile, "They didn't know if he died of lead poisoning or from electric shock he had so many wires on him."

That, of course, was a reference to Halloran being an informant. Sufficiently scared, Solimando told his brother-in-law what happened, and they decided to pay the extortion demand. "It was either that or get killed," Solimando told the jury in Bulger's trial. The first payment was $20,000 in cash which Solimando brought to Triple O's. Another $20,000 was delivered to Bulger in the backseat of a black sedan at the Lancaster Street garage. That's all Solimando could get his hands on immediately. The balance was paid about six months later. Solimando tracked down $215,000 dollars in a Swiss bank account Callahan had, and he got the rest by selling stocks, jewelry, and cars.

And when he was called to testify before a grand jury in 1983, Solimando lied about what had happened. As instructed by Bulger, he swore under oath that the man who extorted money from him was the same man who murdered John Callahan: Bucky Barrett. Bulger told Solimando to tell the story just as it really happened, except to exchange Bulger's name with Barrett's. After all, Barrett was already dead.

About the same time Solimando was making his final payment, Bulger was collecting another $250,000 from a large East Coast pot smuggler named David Lindholm. In 1983 Lindholm successfully brought $72 million worth of marijuana from Columbia to Louisiana. Within five weeks, Lindholm was able to distribute it for $170 million. According to Lindholm's testimony, Bulger wanted a piece of the action, but he had no idea how large the shipment was. He summoned Lindholm to the Marconi Club and demanded a million dollars from him. Lindholm had that kind of money, but he bragged in court that he bluffed Bulger and brought the price down to a quarter-million. First, however, a game of Russian roulette was played.

Bulger had one of his unidentified associates fire a shot past Lindholm's ear to prove the gun worked. He did and it did. Next, all the bullets were dumped on the table and then the gun was loaded with a single bullet.

"The chamber was spun and the gun was pointed at my head," Lindholm said. "The trigger was pulled and it didn't go off."

Bulger paid Lindholm a strange compliment, telling him he had handled himself well, but he also said, "If you piss me off, I'll cut your head off."

Lindholm delivered $60,000 to Jimmy Martorano outside the Boston Aquarium, and another $30,000 to Bulger and Flemmi at the Marconi Club. Over the next two weeks, there were several more payments totaling $160,000. Lindholm continued making rent payments to Bulger for the next six years.

Lindholm told his story convincingly and with an assertive tone. He didn't sound angry, or like a man out for vengeance. He answered the prosecution's questions without hesitation and with appropriate detail. There didn't seem to be much embellishment or hyperbole. In short, he appeared to be credible. The courtroom waited to see if the defense would go after him as a liar and try to poke holes in his story. So, it was surprising to hear Carney ask questions that confirmed the most damaging aspects of the accusations. More than once he put the gun in Bulger's hand. "Bulger took out a gun and told you to answer the questions, didn't he?" "He indicated that you would pay a certain sum of money to him?" "Even with a gun in his hand, you lied to him, didn't you?" "Your arrangement with Mr. Bulger was that you pay him based on the amount of marijuana you sold, right? Each question, and there were several others, sounded like an admission that the story Lindholm told was true. Carney even established further guilt for his client when he introduced new information about various drug deals. "Later he told you that he'd give you twenty-five percent of any drug traffickers that you brought him," Carney stated, and Lindholm agreed.

And when Carney asked Lindholm about the protection Bulger offered to provide, Lindhold gave the jury this unintentional laugh line: "The only person he was protecting us from was him!"

Accusations like this tended to linger in the courtroom. Even if the defense attempted to steamroll past them in a barrage of additional questions and attempted distractions, the reactions that seemed to be straight from the gut were the most memorable. And more often than not, the stories told by a long line of victims claiming to be terrorized by Whitey Bulger went unchallenged.

"He takes the shotgun that was on the table and sticks it in my mouth," Richard Buccheri testified excitedly. Buccheri was introduced to the jury as a seventy-three-year old retired real estate developer with five children, nine grandchildren, and one great grandchild. He had sold Steve Flemmi a condo in Quincy in 1986, and subsequently built the screenhouse adjacent to Flemmi's mother's house. Ironically, that's where he was when Bulger put a gun in his mouth. "Now, he takes out a .45 and puts it to my head," Buccheri explained. "And he says 'If you don't pay me I'm gonna kill you and your family.'"

The reason for Buccheri's plight was that he offered an opinion about a property dispute between a friend of his and Kevin Weeks. The issue involved a fence that was either six inches on Weeks's property, or it wasn't. Buccheri inadvertently picked the wrong side. Bulger was livid that Buccheri didn't favor Weeks in the dispute, but Buccheri didn't even know who Weeks was. He was about to find out.

"Kevin Weeks is my surrogate son!" Bulger shouted as he slammed his hand down hard on the table inside the screenhouse.

It didn't take long for Buccheri to understand what had happened and the situation he was now in. He may not have known who Weeks was, but he knew about Whitey Bulger.

"Richie, you're a stand-up guy," Bulger said while tapping Buccheri on the shoulder with the shotgun. "I'm not gonna kill you now, but it's gonna cost you." Two hundred thousand dollars. That's how much Bulger demanded. Buccheri asked if they'd take a check. To his surprise, the answer was yes. Buccheri made the check out to Flemmi and made it look like the payment was part of a real estate transaction. Weeks claims his end of the shakedown was $50,000, and that Bulger and Flemmi split the rest.

After Buccheri told his story, the defense went after him for past lies and current associations. It turns out he wasn't the innocent grandpa he was initially purported to be.

"You're still friends with James and John Martorano?" co-defense counsel Hank Brennan asked.

"Yes," Buccheri responded.

Suddenly his truthfulness was suspect, and it only got worse when he dodged questions with unbelievable answers. The jury learned that Buccheri had been friends with James and John Martorano since they were all teenagers together. Buccheri admitted to being lifelong friends, and close to the Martorano's families, but he indicated he had no idea what crimes they may have committed.

"At some point you learned what James and John Martorano did for a living?" Brennan asked.

"I really didn't know what they did for a living."

"When you had dinners and you socialized with John Martorano, the subject of what he did for a living never came up?"

"No."

"At some point you learned John Martorano was arrested?"

"I believe so."

There was a lot of movement in the jurors' chairs when Buccheri couldn't even say with certainty that he knew his long-time friend had been arrested, especially since he regularly visited him in jail.

"He was in jail for something," Buccheri equivocated.

"You never inquired why he was in jail?

"No."

"You knew he was a killer?"

"No."

"When he went to Florida, you knew he was a fugitive?

"I don't know if he was or wasn't. He just fled."

"Did you think he was spending time in Disney World?"

The jury sat dumbfounded as Buccheri acknowledged that Martorano had fled, but he wasn't sure why, or if he was a fugitive. Brennan was scoring points, at least until the jury realized that Brennan never challenged Buccheri's account of what happened in the screenhouse. Brennan only showed that Buccheri has questionable friends, and while Buccheri's answers were evasive enough to be considered lies under oath, Brennan didn't even try to prove he was lying about the shotgun in his mouth.

That left an opening for the prosecution to leave another lasting impression with the jury.

"Who were you afraid of?" federal prosecutor Brian Kelly asked on re-direct.

"Whitey Bulger," Buccheri said flatly.

"Is he the one who put the gun in your mouth?"

"Yes, sir."

Bulger's jury listened to these kinds of stories of extortion and terror with fascination. Before them sat an eighty-three-year-old man who appeared harmless and either wrote or doodled on his legal pad hour after hour during his nearly eight week trial. Dozens of witnesses were called to help paint a picture of life in South Boston during the 1970s and 1980s. The individual accounts of people being terrorized by Bulger were so numerous that the only conclusion to draw was that whenever Bulger sniffed out both money and weakness, he pounced. He didn't seem to pass up any opportunity to make a score.

The Bulger jury didn't even hear some of the tales told to previous juries, like when Bernie Weisman fainted while Bulger threatened him with an axe, or when Bulger told a man named Francis Green that he'd cut off his ears and gouge his eyes out. But the jury did hear enough extortion stories to rid all doubt about their validity. The jury was also brought into the world of illegal gambling as a series of bookies and loansharks made their way to the stand to describe the circumstances under which they learned they'd have to pay rent to Bulger.

They heard about Chico Krantz, James Katz, Howard Levinson, Eddie Lewis, William "The Midget" McDonough, Mitchell Zoukoff, Joe Spaziani, David Paul, and Richard Brown—just some of the bookmakers paying Winter Hill upwards of $2,000 a month for many years.

The testimony seemed to corroborate Carney's boast in his opening statement that Jim Bulger made millions of dollars running an organized crime outfit. The ship carrying reasonable doubt regarding Bulger's extortion, drug dealing, and illegal gambling was quickly sailing out of sight.

Solimando's voluntary association with Callahan and Flemmi, Lindholm's criminal record, and Buccheri's friendship with Martorano and his feigned ignorance about Martorano's serial killing history are all examples of warts on a witness. Exposing these guys as underhanded, dishonest criminals who might be willing to lie if it served their own self-interest was like shooting fish in a barrel for Bulger's defense team. Perhaps Kevin Weeks said it best when he was badgered about lies he'd told in the past. "I've been lying all my life," he shouted from the witness stand. "I'm a criminal!"

Weeks was one of the many criminals who seemed so honest in their testimony about their lies and acts of violence that what they said was actually believable.

"I lie to my parents. I lie to my wife. I lie to my girlfriends," Weeks said truthfully.

"What lie would you tell your wife?" Brennan asked.

"That I'm not cheating on her."

"Did she believe you?"

"We're divorced."

"What lie would you tell your girlfriends?"

"That I'm not cheating on them."

Despite Weeks's self-appraisal that he is a liar, a cheat, and a criminal, the jury listened attentively to the man who spent nearly every day with the defendant from 1982 to 1995. Weeks had intimate knowledge of several murders, and he talked openly about them, including his own involvement. He had already served his time, so there was no fear of prosecution.

Weeks had pled guilty to aiding and abetting five murders. The prosecutor recommended he get nine years. The judge sentenced him to six. He was out in five. "The reason I decided to cooperate was because of Stevie Flemmi," Weeks explained why he made the plea deal. "He sent me a letter saying, 'My case is going well. Good luck with yours.' Meaning you're on your own. What was Stevie's next move? All he had left to give up was me and Jim. I made a deal before Stevie did."

"To avoid a life sentence," Carney said.

"Yes, I'd be a fool not to."

"You would be a fool not to," Carney agreed.

"Thank you."

So, Weeks opened up about the murders of Bucky Barrett, John McIntyre, Deborah Hussey, Brian Halloran, and Michael Donahue.

Regarding Barrett, Weeks talked about the safety being on the first time Bulger pulled the trigger, and then Bucky getting shot in the head.

"Who shot him?" Weeks was asked.

"Jim Bulger," came his loud reply into the court microphone.

That was the murder in which Weeks learned that cold water is best for cleaning up blood. Flemmi taught him that.

Regarding McIntyre, Weeks said that after Flemmi announced he was still alive, Bulger shot McIntyre "four or five more times in the face."

Regarding Deborah Hussey, Weeks was surprised and somewhat disturbed when he learned Flemmi and Bulger were going to kill her. "She was a girl," he quietly protested. "She wasn't a criminal. I didn't think anything was going to come of it. I went upstairs to use the bathroom. As I came down the stairs, I heard a thud. I saw Jim Bulger had her on the ground and was choking her. It took about four minutes until she was dead. Her eyes had rolled up and her lips were blue." Weeks finished the story by saying that Flemmi put his head on Deborah's chest and determined she was still alive. "So, he put a rope around her neck with a stick and started twisting it."

Regarding Halloran and Donahue, Weeks told the jury he was the lookout who called Bulger on a two-way radio to tell him Halloran was leaving the Pier Grill Restaurant, and he watched Bulger shoot Halloran with enough bullets to make his body dance on the ground.

Weeks admitted to moving the bodies from 799 East Third to a pre-dug burial site behind Florian Hall. He said when they dug the holes earlier in the day, Bulger left a twenty-dollar bill partly showing from underneath a rock, so that if the twenty were missing when they returned, they'd know if someone had been there. The twenty was right where Bulger left it when they came back that night with the bodies, so they went ahead with the burial.

And regarding Debbie Davis, Weeks said that Flemmi told him she was strangled, but he didn't say who strangled her. It was somewhat disappointing testimony for Steve Davis to hear, because he knew that it left room for some doubt in the minds of the jurors. They would only be left with Flemmi's version of the event, and that was highly suspect. But Steve Davis was impressed with Weeks's overall testimony and with their encounter after court.

"I just want you to know I didn't have anything to do with your sister's murder," Weeks told Davis during a break in the trial. "I didn't even know her." Weeks didn't team up with Bulger until a year or so after Debbie Davis disappeared. Steve Davis was stunned by Weeks's approach, and he was unprepared to respond. Weeks abruptly walked away, and it took a few seconds before Steve called out to him, "Kevin," he shouted, and Weeks turned around. "Thanks."

Weeks nodded and ducked back into the courtroom. His testimony still had a long way to go. He returned to the stand and said that two days before Christmas in 1994, John Connolly led him into the cooler at the variety store next to Rotary Liquors and told him the feds were about to pinch Bulger and Flemmi. Weeks sent a message to Bulger's pager, and then met with Bulger and Theresa Stanley, and drove them to Nieman Marcus. While Theresa shopped for shoes, Weeks told Bulger about the impending indictments. Bulger calmly received the news, and made plans to leave town with Theresa. This contradicted Jay Carney's opening statement in which he said Bulger heard about the indictments in a radio news report.

Weeks continued with a detailed account of Bulger's return to Boston when he dropped Theresa off in Hingham, and then met Weeks and Catherine Greig at Malibu Beach in Dorchester. Weeks saw Bulger again in the spring of 1995 in New York, and again in the summer of 1996 in Chicago. Prior to that second trip, Weeks took pictures of Whitey's brother, Jackie, and made false IDs for Whitey. A second set of IDs was required, however, because Bulger didn't like the first ones. The new set was delivered to Bulger in New York.

It was the thirty-first time Weeks had told these stories under oath. There were several different grand juries, depositions, and trials since he made his plea deal. He was required to testify whenever called, and he was required to tell the truth. He either did, or his lies were exceedingly consistent, because Carney couldn't find any discrepancies in his thirty-one testimonies. Weeks may have been a thug, a thief, and an accessory to murder, but he was tough to discredit as a witness. So, Carney took a different tack.

"During the years you were with Jim Bulger he was involved in all sorts of crimes," Carney stated. "And these crimes involved extorting people?"

"Correct," Weeks said.

"Money laundering?"

"Correct."

"Loansharking?"

"Correct."

"Drug dealing?"

"Correct."

"And on occasions crimes of violence?"

"Correct."

It was such an odd line of questioning that one might think Carney was laying a trap of some kind. If so, the trap never snapped on its prey. Weeks continued unflustered with the story of how he staked out the house of *Boston Herald* reporter Howie Carr, who was a long-time critic of Bulger's. Weeks's intention was to shoot Carr with a long-range rifle, but the plan was thwarted when Carr came out of the house with his daughter. He also said under cross examination that he was with John Connolly at the Top of the Hub restaurant when Connolly showed him Bulger's informant file.

"When you were with Jim Bulger you learned that what he hated above all else was informants," Carney stated.

"We killed people for being informants," Weeks agreed.

"The culture in South Boston was that you never rat on your friends, or your enemies," Carney said. "If you have a problem, you take it to the street."

"Correct."

It seemed as though Carney was intimating that Weeks was a rat for testifying against Bulger, the man who mentored him, and the man who helped him earn, by his own account, nearly $2 million during their twelve years together. But Weeks inferred something else from the new line of questioning. "You can't rat on a rat," he said.

"What would you do if someone called you a rat to your face?" Carney asked brazenly.

"Why don't you call me that outside when it's just you and me, and see what I do?"

Nonplused, but not thrown off guard, Carney pressed Weeks on his lack of loyalty. He was able to get Weeks to admit that he was hoping Bulger would never be caught, "so we wouldn't be in this circus right now," which suggested Weeks might be willing to lie about someone who would never be charged, much the same way Bulger had Solimando testify against the already deceased Bucky Barrett. But Carney may have gone too far when he suggested Weeks was the winner in all of his because he cut such a sweet deal and only served five years in prison.

"What did I win?" Weeks shouted with a surprisingly disdainful tone. "What did I win? Five people are dead. Yeah, it bothers me. We killed people who were rats and I had the two biggest rats next to me!"

This prompted Bulger to speak for the first time in nearly a month. The jurors may not have ever heard him speak before this moment, but they heard him now, and they heard him loud and clear.

"You suck!" he shouted at Weeks.

"Fuck you, okay," Weeks shouted right back.

"Fuck you, too!"

"What do you want to do!" Weeks threw his arms open wide assuming the posture of someone inviting a physical altercation. Bulger never moved, but he glared at Weeks with equal parts rage and disappointment. His protégé had not only turned on him, he had just threatened him. In fact, all his old so-called friends had turned on him. His brother, Jackie, was in the courtroom most days, but his brother, Billy, never showed. The women in his life had either married, moved on, or been incarcerated. Bulger sat at the defense table flanked by his two lawyers, no doubt realizing that they were two of the very few people still on his side—because they were paid to be there. For all intents and purposes Bulger was alone in the world. It was just him, his evil thoughts, his delusional self-aggrandizement, and his doodles. It was beginning to sink in that this is where the grand life of an organized crime boss was going to end.

Once U.S. District Court Judge Denise J. Casper settled down the courtroom after Weeks's and Bulger's cockfight, Carney paused and asked one final question for the day. It was intended to insult the witness, and leave the jury a lasting impression of his character, but it wildly missed its mark.

"It doesn't bother you that you killed those people, does it?" Carney asked.

"I didn't kill those people," Weeks reminded him, "Your client killed those people. I was there. We're all guilty."

CHAPTER ELEVEN

Steve Davis Takes the Stand

The life and times of Whitey Bulger were being exposed in Courtroom 11 by a parade of witnesses with varying degrees of credibility. Hundreds of hours, thousands of pages of testimony, and several hundred photos and other exhibits created a mountain of information for the jurors to consider. In mostly candid and unvarnished tones, they heard outrageous and scurrilous tales of heinous violence and wanton behavior.

The jurors learned, for example, that drug dealer Joe Murray wasn't allowed to retire until he gave Bulger $500,000. They negotiated the buyout on a bench outside the New England Aquarium on Boston's waterfront in 1988. Murray returned a few days later with the cash in a duffel bag.

Another drug dealer named Hobart Willis paid $250,000 "not to get killed." Still another, Paul Moore, paid Bulger nearly that much every year for a decade.

"Why did he have to be paid?" prosecutor Brian Kelly asked Moore.

"He's the boss," was Moore's simple reply.

Some of the stories went back forty years, like when Frank Capizzi described what happened when Al "Bud" Plummer gave him a ride home on the night of March 19, 1973.

"It was like a firing squad hit us," the seventy-eight-year-old Capizzi told the jury. "For about two and a half minutes about one hundred slugs hit the automobile. I'd been hit in the head and could feel warm blood running down my neck. I said, 'Bud, come on.' I put my hand up and my hand went into his neck where his head should have been."

The jury also heard from John Martorano that he and Bulger were the shooters who killed Plummer. Martorano said they were after Al Notarangeli, who was suspected of killing one of the Mafia's bookies. They shot up the wrong car that night and again less than two weeks later.

When sixty-three-year-old Diane Sussman took the stand, jurors had no idea they were about to hear some of the most dramatic testimony in the trial. Sussman, they learned, was a mother of two, married for thirty years, living in Los Angeles, and working in school business administration. She didn't seem to belong at this trial, but she had an unexpected tragic love story to tell.

In March 1973 Sussman was living in Brighton, a neighborhood of Boston. She was dating a bartender at Mother's Cafe named Louie Lapiana. Sussman had been out celebrating her twenty-third birthday with her girlfriends. At the end of the night, her friends dropped her off at Mother's where she waited for Louie's shift to end. Another bartender, Michael Milano, volunteered to drive them both home in his brand new Mercedes, the same make and model car as Al Notarangeli's. When Milano stopped at a red light, the car was suddenly hit with a hail of gunfire.

Sussman was wounded. Milano died on the way to the hospital. And Lapiana lived the next twenty-eight years as a quadriplegic on a respirator. Sussman tearfully told the jury of how she stayed with Lapiana for two years in Boston, and when she picked up and moved to Los Angeles, Lapiana went there, too. He was part of her life. When she married and had children, he became part of her husband's and children's lives until he died in 2001. The jury was moved to tears listening to Sussman talk about her love and affection for her dear friend Louie.

"Who do you believe shot Michael Milano?" Carney asked as sympathetically as he could.

"That would be speculation," Sussman said. "In my mind, I do know. But that's for me." She refrained from firing accusations at Bulger, perhaps because she was under oath and didn't know with absolute certainty who fired those machine guns at Milano's car that night, but when she left the courthouse she was more free to speak her mind, and she did. "This is a circus," she told the media, and as she held up a picture of Louie on a respirator, she added, "This is how Louie lived for twenty-eight years and nobody cared." Her anger began to rise, and finally she said of Bulger, "He's a no good son-of-a-bitch, and honestly, I wish I could just shoot him. I'd shoot both of them [Bulger and Martorano]. Unfortunately, we don't live our life that way."

The jury didn't get to hear Diane Sussman's suspicions or see her raw emotion, but they saw plenty of grief and some anger on display during the trial, as the prosecution called several victims' family members.

Sixty-seven-year-old Donald Milano cried nearly uncontrollably on the stand as he recalled hearing on the radio that his older brother had been killed. Sixty-one-year-old Debra Scully told the jury she was carrying Bill O'Brien's child when he was killed on Morrissey Boulevard in 1973.

Patricia Donahue, the widow of Michael Donahue told the jury her recollections of the day her husband fatefully gave Brian Halloran a ride. Patricia heard retired medical examiner Richard Evans say that Michael was shot four times, and that one "bullet went through the left side of the brain." Michael was killed instantly, but Patricia's anger has lasted over thirty years. "I don't understand why all these people who were involved in my husband's death are walking around like nothing ever happened," Patricia testified. "I don't think it's fair, and I don't understand why the government let that happen."

Patricia, of course, knows now that the government, specifically the FBI and special agent John Morris, not only let it happen, they initiated it. Morris is the one who tipped off Connolly, who then told Bulger that Halloran was cooperating with investigators about the murder of Roger Wheeler. Morris testified that he feels the blood is on his hands, that he's responsible for the Halloran and Donahue murders. While testifying, Morris looked directly at Patricia Donahue and her sons Michael and Tommy, and said, "I don't ask for your forgiveness, but I do want to express my sincere apology for things I may have done and for things I didn't do. Not a day in my life has gone by that I haven't thought about this. Not a day in my life has gone by that I haven't prayed that God give you comfort and blessing for the pain you suffered. I am truly sorry. I don't ask for your forgiveness. That's too much. But I do acknowledge it publicly."

Morris's words were a rare poignant moment in the trial. They appeared to be genuine, heartfelt, and unrehearsed. But the apology lost some of its meaning when the jury was reminded that it was only three weeks after Halloran and Donahue were killed that Morris flew his mistress down to be with him in Georgia, and that Bulger paid for her plane ticket.

Morris's apology was not accepted by the Donahues. "His tears and his apologies don't mean crap to me or my family," Tommy Donahue told reporters. "I thought it was a complete joke. He can actually take his apology and shove it." Patricia Donahue, still wearing a necklace her husband gave her for her thirtieth birthday, also dismissed Morris's apology. "Those words didn't mean anything to me," she said. "While he's getting promotions, I'm mourning my husband. So, obviously, those 'sorries' didn't mean anything."

Steve Davis empathized with each of the family members. He knew their pain and their anger, because he carried it with him each day of the trial. It was difficult to hear the impact of Bulger's acts on so many people. It was equally difficult to hear the details of his sister's death, and to see the photos of the discovery of her body.

Dr. Ann Marie Mires, a Massachusetts state forensic anthropologist, described the search for Debbie's body beneath the Neponset River Bridge. Dr. Mires was there when the backhoe scraped the top of Debbie's grave and latched on to the ropes that were used to tie up her body in a green, plastic bag. The backhoe pulled the ropes and exposed what was left of the beautiful, young woman: her skull and other bones.

Dr. Mires speculated Debbie's body was buried at low tide, and that her skull was damaged post-mortem due to the knots in the ropes swaying with the waves and hitting her repeatedly. "We identified the body to be Debra Davis," Dr. Mires said. "The body position was tightly flexed in a fetal position on her side. There is post-mortem damage to the skull. The frontal view of the skull shows no teeth."

This is my sister they're talking about, thought Steve.

Retired medical examiner, Richard Evans, could testify only to the fact that homicidal violence was involved in Debbie's death. He said, "It's not possible to know what type of violence that might have been. There are no real clues in the bone that would answer that question." Evans said it's possible Debbie was strangled, but he couldn't testify to that with a "reasonable medical degree of certainty."

Steve teared up when a photograph of Debbie's skull was shown. He had never seen it before. There was an outline of a face, and some hair had been preserved. The gruesome photo and Steve's imagination combined to bring about an image of his sister as both a beautiful, young woman, and a discarded victim.

The full range of Steve's emotions was on display throughout the trial. When he was sad, he cried. When he was incredulous, he rolled his eyes and folded his arms across his burly chest. When he was angry, he stormed out, and he did that more than once. And when he was nervous, like the day he was called to testify, he spoke softly and deliberately. Asked to describe his recollections of the day Debbie went missing, Steve said, "My mother called me and told me something was wrong. She had put a hundred calls into a beeper Steve [Flemmi] had given Debbie. [Flemmi] called my mother back and said, 'She took off.'"

"Did you ever see your sister again?" the defense asked.

"No, not until yesterday," Steve replied referring to the autopsy photos.

Bulger's defense attorneys didn't cross-examine too many of the victims' family members, but Jay Carney did have a few questions for Steve. He started by laying the foundation that Flemmi bought Debbie expensive gifts and treated her as his possession, and he eventually intimated that Flemmi was the jealous type. Carney was attempting to show that it was Flemmi who had a motive to kill Debbie. "Was Steve Flemmi jealous if she spoke to another man?" he asked Steve.

"Yes."

"You learned in 1981 that Debbie wanted to end the relationship with Steve Flemmi."

"It was a rocky road with them. Yes."

"After your sister's disappearance, Steve Flemmi came around the house."

"Yes."

"He said he was doing everything he could do to find her?"

"That's what he said."

"Did you believe him?"

"I never believed it from the beginning when she never answered my mother's calls. He advised my mother not to call the FBI or local police. I told her not to listen to him. We all felt, my mother felt, it was his reputation. It was all bullshit. It was a bunch of crap."

Finally, Carney gave Steve a chance to speak from the heart about his sister, but he framed his question in a way that cast more suspicion, or at least blame, on Flemmi rather than Bulger. "Is there anything else you want to tell the jury about who your sister was before she met Stevie Flemmi?"

"She was a beautiful, young woman. She had no enemies— except for two." He was referring to Bulger and Flemmi, though it may not have been clear to the jury at the time. "Everybody that met her loved her," Steve continued. "She was full of life. She was my best friend growing up."

The jury had learned during the first few weeks of the trial that Debbie Davis *might* have been strangled. Flemmi said Bulger had killed her, but Kevin Weeks's testimony in this trial left room for doubt whether it was Bulger or Flemmi who had done it. The jury also heard the defense slip a question in to Dickie O'Brien that he may have answered without any real consideration.

"You were uncomfortable with Steve Flemmi?"

"Yes."

"You were aware that he killed his girlfriend, Debbie Davis?"

"Yes."

And then the jury heard from Debbie's own brother that she was about to dump Steve Flemmi, thus giving the admitted killer a motive to kill again. It was time for the jury to meet Steve Flemmi.

CHAPTER TWELVE

The Prosecution's Star Witness

There was no consoling Steven Rakes on the afternoon of Tuesday, July 16, 2013. The prosecution's case had been steam-rolling along for five weeks, and Rakes was about to become a part of it. No longer afraid of Whitey Bulger, Rakes couldn't wait to get on the stand and outline in great detail how Bulger had strong-armed him out of his South Shore Liquor Mart in 1983. Rakes was a constant in the courtroom throughout the trial, and he had been sitting there when Kevin Weeks told the jury the takeover of the liquor store was "not your typical extortion." Weeks said Rakes had agreed to sell the store, and then tried to back out of the deal—which Bulger wouldn't permit.

"Kevin continues to lie," Rakes told reporters, "because that's what he has to do. My liquor store was never for sale. Never, never, never! He's got his day up on that stand, and then I'll have my day."

But Rakes never had his day in court. After telling friends that when he got his chance to testify he was going to drop a bombshell, one was dropped on him. Prosecutors pulled him aside on July 16 and told him they wouldn't be calling him as a witness after all. Rakes was devastated.

It's likely Rakes was told his testimony would not only contradict and undermine Weeks's version of events, but it would also damage Weeks's already tenuous credibility. And prosecutors needed the jury to believe Weeks on several other allegations. It didn't make sense for the prosecution to call two witnesses with divergent stories. The jury wouldn't know who to believe.

Rakes left prosecutors that afternoon and forcefully swung open the courthouse doors. He instantly felt the wall of heat outside the building, but he plowed right through it. Rakes always walked quickly and purposefully, so when he blew past reporters and made a beeline for the parking lot, no one would have suspected he was upset. But when he made eye contact with Steve Davis and kept going without a joke, or a comment, or an observation about the day's proceedings, Steve knew something was wrong. Davis called out to Rakes who reluctantly stopped. Shuffling his feet and jingling his car keys in his pocket, Rakes told Davis he wasn't going to testify. Davis tried to comfort his friend, but the conversation was too short. Rakes had somewhere to be.

Rakes left the courthouse just after one o'clock and drove to Waltham, a suburb west of Boston. He pulled into a McDonald's restaurant and met an old business associate named William Camuti. Camuti had arrived first and greeted Rakes with an iced coffee. What happened next would send a shockwave through this already dramatic trial.

Steve Davis was unaware anything was wrong, but he was a little concerned when Rakes didn't return his calls Tuesday night, and that concern grew when he noticed Rakes missing from court on Wednesday. "That's not like him," Davis told his lunch companions on Wednesday afternoon. "He's upset, but I know he wanted to see this thing through to the end." Davis was dining at Strega in Boston with a CNN film crew working on a documentary about the Bulger victims' families. The restaurant's owner, Nick Verano, brought over a feast and Steve ate voraciously. "The only thing better than great food," Steve announced, "is great food on the house!" It was a great day for Steve, but he worried again when Rakes didn't return another phone call.

Thursday, July 18, was the day Steve Flemmi was scheduled to testify, but his highly anticipated appearance was overshadowed by shocking news: Steve Rakes was dead. His body was found in a wooded area just off a jogging path in Lincoln, Massachusetts. He was wearing the same clothes he had on Tuesday when he was last seen at the courthouse. Police said there was no wallet, no ID, and no cellphone found with the body. There were no signs of physical trauma. And his car was found in a McDonald's parking lot about seven miles away.

Speculation wavered between two theories: Rakes had committed suicide, or he had been murdered. The timing was certainly suspicious. Right in the middle of the Whitey Bulger trial a key witness mysteriously turned up dead in what appeared to be another body dump. Even though Rakes wasn't going to be called to testify, a would-be assassin might not have known that, and Rakes had often talked tough in the media calling Bulger a coward and a rat. Maybe a little Southie revenge was behind Rakes's death.

As for suicide, Steve Davis dismissed that out of hand. The Steven Rakes he knew loved life. Rakes was a health nut who loved to ride his bike and spend time at the beach. He bragged about successful business deals and having a lot of money. And while Rakes was undoubtedly upset and angry about not getting to testify, he still wanted to watch Bulger go down. "He had a lot to live for," Davis said.

The mystery lingered as Steve Flemmi took the stand. Flemmi arrived in the courtroom before the jurors returned from the standard mid-morning break. Flemmi glared at Bulger, who only glanced back and returned to writing on his legal pad.

While Flemmi testified, the jury saw before them a seventy-nine-year-old man whose shoulders had narrowed and hunched over time. His hair was still thick and black with only slight touches of gray. He wore glasses and a beige lightweight jacket zipped up nearly to the top. Responding to questions from Assistant U.S. Attorney Fred Wyshack, Flemmi told the jury about his plea bargain in which he had admitted to ten murders, extortion, shakedowns, narcotics distribution, money laundering, numerous firearms violations, and yes, perjury. And for admitting all of this, Flemmi had avoided the death penalty and received a life sentence instead, with an additional thirty-year sentence on the gun charges.

"Life plus thirty," Wyshack said.

"Yes," Flemmi confirmed. Flemmi sat comfortably with his arm draped over the chair, or at times, with his hands folded like a schoolboy in front of him. He seemed relaxed while the prosecution asked him a long series of obviously rehearsed questions, and he answered them directly. He told the jury he first met Bulger on one occasion in 1969, and then spent nearly every day with him from the spring of 1974 until the Christmas of 1994. They hadn't seen each other since then because Flemmi was in jail, and Bulger was on the run.

"What was the nature of your relationship during those twenty years?" Wyshack asked.

"Strictly criminal," was Flemmi's quick reply.

"Was Mr. Bulger an FBI informant?"

"Yes."

"Were you present with Mr. Bulger when he gave information to the FBI?"

"Hundreds of times."

The questions and answers were fired back and forth with a rhythmic cadence. Flemmi's responses were so immediate that his first word occasionally stepped on Wyshack's last. This dance between the prosecutor and the star witness lasted only about fifteen minutes before the court adjourned for the day, but the jury was left with one final impression to consider overnight when Flemmi mouthed "You mouthfucker" at Bulger as he stepped down from the witness stand. The expletive wasn't audible, but it was seen by many, including a few jurors. Bulger mumbled something back, to which Flemmi responded, "Really?" Flemmi's silent affront was a detrimental moment for the prosecution because the jury now knew to consider Flemmi's hatred for Bulger when he testified. And Flemmi would testify for four days.

Flemmi was the prosecution's most important witness for several reasons. He was Bulger's closest partner at the top of the Winter Hill Gang. He could corroborate the testimonies of Weeks and Martorano. And his plea deal still resulted in life in prison. While Weeks and Martorano could be suspected of embellishing stories to get their sentences lightened, Flemmi would never again be a free man. He'd get nothing from his testimony, except perhaps the satisfaction of sticking it to Bulger.

Back on the stand Friday morning, Flemmi quickly summarized his life of crime. He explained that he had started as a bookmaker and a loanshark operating out of Roxbury in the late 1950s. Then he rather indifferently described his role in a long list of murders. It was presented almost like an oral quiz with Wyshack tossing out a name, and Flemmi explaining how the person died.

"Leo Lowery."

"My brother Jimmy killed him. I helped get rid of the body."

"William Train."

"Johnny Murray may have killed him. I helped get rid of the body."

"George Ash."

"My brother Jimmy killed him. I helped move the body."

"Stephen Hughes and Sam Lindenbalm."

"Howie Winter killed them. I cleaned up the shells out of the car with Frank Salemme."

"Wimpy Bennett."

"I shot him."

"Where?"

"In the head."

"What location?"

"In a garage over in Roxbury."

"Who buried the body?"

"Myself, Joe MacDonald, and Jimmy Sims. They didn't like Wimpy."

Flemmi rattled off names and places as if he were flipping through a photo album and reminiscing about the good old days. And there were many more recollections. Tommy Timmons was killed by the Mafia in Frank Salemme's home, and because Frank's wife was upstairs, they strangled him quietly instead of shooting him. Larry Baione and Salemme buried the body. Wimpy Bennett, Flemmi said, was buried near a gun club in Hopkinton. Walter Bennett was buried there, too, after Frank Salemme and Peter Poulos killed him. But the third brother, William Bennett, never made it to Hopkinton. After

Sonny Shields shot and killed him, William fell out of the car and into a snow bank.

There wasn't an ounce of remorse or sympathy in Flemmi's tone. When he described the attempted murder of attorney John Fitzgerald in 1968, he said he was down the street when the car exploded, and added simply that "Fitzgerald had his leg blown off." There was no discernible shrug of Flemmi's shoulders, but the intonation in his voice suggested an apathy that was downright odious. And as the listing of murder victims continued, jurors may have wondered how long it would go on.

"There were probably about sixty gangland slayings in the sixties," Flemmi estimated. "The gang war was used as an excuse." This ballpark approximation so callously uttered revealed an even larger body count than any charges or convictions had taken into account. Flemmi had originally admitted to ten murders in his plea agreement. Bulger was accused of killing nineteen people. Now, this estimate was twice that sum total.

Flemmi next told the jury that FBI Special Agent Paul Rico tipped him off about the impending indictment against him in the Fitzgerald car bombing case. So, Flemmi fled to Montreal where he worked at a newspaper under a false name. The newspaper didn't pay much, but Flemmi said John Martorano and Brian Halloran traveled up to see him and dropped off "some money." Flemmi didn't specify how much, but it was enough to keep him on the lam for five years.

Flemmi's oddly nostalgic jaunt to the past also included stories of extortion, like the time in the late 1970s when John Connolly gave Bulger crime photographs of a multiple murder scene, and Bulger used those photos to convince a real estate developer named Ted Berenson that he killed the people in the photos, and that he'd kill Berenson, too. Berenson then handed over $60,000 for his life.

Flemmi further bragged that through the years a marijuana dealer named Frank Lapere paid Winter Hill a total of more than a million dollars. Twice in 1983 Lapere's payments of $25,000 went directly to Connolly. "I'm one of the gang!" Connolly had said gleefully at the time. Wyshack asked Flemmi if Connolly was, in fact, part of the gang.

"Yes," Flemmi said.

Connolly wasn't the only crooked cop. Flemmi also told the jury about payments to FBI agents Paul Rico, Dennis Condon, and John Morris. There was also a lieutenant in the Massachusetts State Police named Richard Schneiderhan who Flemmi said was paid a thousand dollars a month from 1978 until the 1990s.

Steve Davis grew uneasy as he sat and listened to the accusations of extensive government corruption. His sister Debbie was dead because if it. Steve and his family had proven that in court. The guilty parties were Bulger, Flemmi, and the FBI, and not necessarily in that order.

"Were you in love with her?" Steve heard Wyshack ask Flemmi about Debbie.

"I loved her," he said, but quickly attached a sophomoric addendum. "But I wasn't *in* love with her."

Steve Davis merely considered that one of the many lies Flemmi told under oath. Flemmi, who was testifying in his eighteenth criminal proceeding, then retold the same story about how Debbie deduced he and Bulger were informants. The timeline went from March when Flemmi says he "blurted out" that he was going to see FBI Agent Connolly. In May 1981 Ronnie Davis was killed in prison, and Debbie told Flemmi to use his FBI connection to find out what had happened. During the summer, Flemmi told Bulger that Debbie knew about Connolly, and she may have told one of her brothers, who according to Flemmi, was an informant. And by September 17 Bulger had convinced Flemmi that Debbie needed to die.

"I eventually agreed," Flemmi said. "And it happened. It's affected me, and it's going to affect me until the day I die."

The gruesome details of Debbie's murder provided by Flemmi always upset Steve Davis. He'd heard them many times either from Flemmi's testimonies or various news reports. But what upset him even more on this day was when Flemmi said Debbie's brother was an informant, but he didn't specify which brother. Steve was beyond vexed that anyone might think Flemmi was referring to him. When court adjourned for the day, Steve strode right up to the prosecution attorneys Wyshack and Brian Kelly, and demanded they get Flemmi to clarify his testimony the next day. It was not an important fact related to the trial, but it was extremely important to Steve, and that made it important to the prosecution. In addition to putting Bulger away forever, the prosecution was also very interested in offering some comfort to the victims' families.

After that, Steve stepped outside the courthouse and walked directly to the collection of microphones attached to a thin stand, and told local and national reporters that Flemmi was referring to his brother, Mickey Davis, not him. Steve went home and watched as many of the news reports as he could and was somewhat satisfied that they all included his disaffirmation. But he didn't sleep well that night—or the next two nights. Flemmi's vague accusation occurred on a Friday. Steve had to wait until Monday for the record to be cleared.

Wyshack obliged Steve's request, and the very first question he asked Flemmi on Monday morning was, "Which Davis brother were you referring to when you said one was doing drugs and may be an informant?"

Flemmi knew the question was coming, so his answer was surprisingly disconnected, perhaps intentionally so. He leaned into the microphone, and said very clearly, "Steven Davis." There was a split second of shock, and then Flemmi began to say, "He's not the one I was referring to . . ."

His response was drowned out by Steve's instinctive explosion. "That's a lie!" he said rising to his feet. "That's a fucking lie!"

"It wasn't you I was referring to," Flemmi said innocently to Steve, who was already being restrained by a security guard. Judge Denise Casper also directed her remarks to Steve, simultaneously asking him and telling him to settle down. "I need you to be respectful of these proceedings," she said. "You can stay here, if you can do that."

Steve nodded to her and sat back down, and again Flemmi said, "I wasn't referring to Steven Davis. I was referring to his brother, Mickey. I apologize for that remark."

It was hard to tell if Flemmi was feigning sincerity to cover up a malicious little trick he had just pulled to get under Steve's skin, or if he was honestly confused when he first heard the question. Either way, with another nod of his head Steve accepted the apology, but he couldn't help but think it was the first time Flemmi ever apologized to him for anything, including the deaths of his father, his brother, and at least one sister.

Despite being allowed to stay in the courtroom, Steve Davis left a few minutes later. He had been agitated by the angry exchange, and he needed to get out and walk around. "I blacked out when I heard my name," Davis told reporters. "I was defending who I am and what I represent, and what I'm about. He called me a rat, an informant, and I'd take a bullet before I'd ever incriminate anyone."

He returned to the courtroom to see Flemmi continue to rat on his former friend, Whitey Bulger. He also noticed Flemmi mumble some responses and appear disoriented on others. Steve drew the conclusion that Flemmi had also been disturbed by the verbal altercation, or according to Steve, he was "off his meds."

Right in the middle of telling the story of John McIntyre's murder, it was clear Flemmi still had the Davis brothers on his mind. "He shot him in the head," Flemmi testified, and then, "Davis, both of them." His voice trailed off. His confusion was evident. He suddenly appeared like an actor who was forgetting his lines, or saying them in the wrong order.

When asked about Deborah Hussey, he said, "She was my girlfriend." Hussey was the stepdaughter with whom he had an ongoing sexual relationship, though he denied it with semantics.

"Did you have a sexual relationship with her?"

"Not intercourse," he said with both pride and indignation.

"How long did it take to kill her?" Wyshack said referring only to Deborah Hussey.

"It didn't take long," Flemmi said, adding, "They were two fragile women." Flemmi seemed to be inadvertently connecting the murders of Deborah Hussey and Debbie Davis, but undoubtedly the jury would connect them purposefully. The stories were nearly identical. Both women were sexual partners of Flemmi. Bulger didn't like either of them. Flemmi said he wanted to send both of them away, but Bulger convinced him they should be killed. Both were strangled in houses on East Third Street. And both were buried just outside of South Boston. It's possible that the jury would either believe or disbelieve both stories equally. And since Kevin Weeks and Flemmi told the same story about Deborah Hussey, Flemmi's lone version of the Deborah Davis murder might have more credibility. But the jury would have to dismiss the relevant proximity of Debbie's murder being so close to her plans to leave Flemmi for Gustavo in Mexico. Flemmi still had the stronger motive, but as the jury would find out during cross-examination, Flemmi was not above perjuring himself.

Co-defense counsel Hank Brennan handled the cross-examination, and he went right after Flemmi about his sexual relationship with his stepdaughter, Deborah Hussey. It was a successful tactic on two fronts. First, he let the jury see that Flemmi the murderer was even more vile as a sex offender, and second, he made Flemmi look foolish by catching him in a series of lies.

"You never let Deborah Hussey sit on your knee and read stories to her?" Brennan asked.

"Of course not, no," Flemmi said as if the thought disgusted him. "I didn't even do that with my own children."

Brennan approached him with a transcript from the McIntyre civil suit and showed Flemmi that he testified that Deborah used to sit on his knee. That was Flemmi's first lie.

"When you ask me about the murders, there's no lies," Flemmi said in an effort to defend himself. But as his testimony continued, his own words revealed his depravity. By the time Brennan was through with the Hussey issue alone, he had successfully exposed Flemmi's soul, and eviscerated it.

"Is it hard for you to accept that you strangled someone who called you Daddy?" Brennan asked.

"I didn't strangle her."

"She called you Daddy, didn't she?"

"Mr. Brennan, I didn't strangle her."

"Did little Deborah Hussey call you Daddy?"

"She thought I was her Daddy. Probably did. I'm saying she did."

The difficulty Flemmi had simply acknowledging that Deborah called him Daddy was noticeably odd. He was no longer on script, and his accounts were being challenged. Brennan continued by asking when Flemmi had begun sexually abusing his stepdaughter.

"Are you talking about intercourse or oral sex?" Flemmi asked insinuating that one was worse than the other. "I never inflicted any abuse on her. That was consensual."

"So your daughter who called you Daddy consented to have sex with you?" Brennan followed up.

"Mr. Brennan, that's a whole different ballgame. Different time. If you want to bring it back to the early years, you're way off the wall there." Flemmi went on to explain that after he came back from being a fugitive, he didn't view Deborah as a child anymore. She was a "whole different person" to him. He said there was no longer a father-daughter relationship.

"At what point did you become attracted to her?" Brennan asked.

"I wasn't attracted to her," Flemmi replied.

"When you decided to inflict sex upon her . . ."

"Did you say inflict?" Flemmi interrupted. "Consensual."

"When you decided to have . . ."

"Two occasions," Flemmi interrupted again. "I regret it. It was a moment of weakness." It seemed to be important to Flemmi that the jury believe he only had Deborah perform oral sex on him twice, as if somehow that would be less offensive.

Brennan moved on and found another lie in Flemmi's previous testimony, this one even more significant than the first. In the McIntyre lawsuit in 2006, Flemmi said Bulger strangled

Deborah Hussey with a rope. Two weeks later, when he was being deposed for the *Florida v Connolly* criminal case, Flemmi said he thought Bulger "used his hands" when he strangled Deborah Hussey. Flemmi weakly defended himself by claiming he was in a "state of anxiety at the time" of the murder.

Brennan exposed the same kind of inconsistency in Flemmi's testimony relevant to Debbie Davis. At times he had testified Bulger grabbed her around the throat with his hands, but under oath in 2009, he agreed it was "almost like a headlock."

"Where's the inconsistencies?" Flemmi asked.

Brennan spent the better part of a day hammering Flemmi with questions about the murders of Debbie Davis and Deborah Hussey. He successfully linked them together, and perhaps was also successful in showing the jury that Flemmi was more likely the guilty party in both. Curiously, Flemmi admitted to being an active participant before each of the murders by luring the women to the houses, and again after each of the murders by pulling out their teeth, stripping their bodies, and burying them in unmarked graves. "It didn't make sense to mark the grave," Flemmi explained.

Even though he had been there before, during, and after the two murders, Flemmi continued to pin the blame on Bulger. In order to accept this, the jury would have to believe an odd dichotomy existed in Flemmi's character. He was the co-leader of a violent criminal organization, an unremorseful murderer, and a pedophile capable of unspeakable acts, yet he was subservient to Bulger and was coerced into killing his stepdaughter and girlfriend.

"That murder could have been prevented with one word on Bulger's part," Flemmi said, referring to Deborah Hussey. "He could have said stop."

"He could have said stop when you had that stick and that rope and you continued to twist and twist and twist it," Brennan responded emphatically.

"All he had to say was pass, four little letters, P-A-S-S, and I would have been so happy. That would have been the end of it.

"Did you defend her in that house?"

"She was murdered. He could have prevented it. He could have said pass. She'd be alive today. That would have been the same thing with Debra Davis. He was in control," Flemmi said, raising his voice. His body didn't move any more than the inch as he leaned into the microphone to drive home his point. He looked Brennan in the eye as if they were the only two people in the room. "I could have done it if I wanted to. I didn't need any other witnesses."

Brennan wasn't through with Flemmi. He asked him how many teeth he pulled out of his stepdaughter's mouth. He accused Flemmi of enjoying his reputation as a murderer. He mocked Flemmi for complaining to Judge Wolf during the 1998 hearings that Walpole prison was unpleasant. Flemmi had whined then and again in front of Bulger's jury that the food was so bad, he'd lost thirty-five pounds. He wasn't allowed to listen to the radio, watch TV, or read books, and the other inmates were calling him a rat. Of all the adjectives the jury may have already assigned to Flemmi, they could now add "pathetic."

"You don't like the word rat, do you?" Brennan asked.

"I don't think anyone likes it. I don't think Mr. Bulger likes it either."

"In prison there's a word that's worse than murderer," Brennan went on. "It's pedophile."

"You want to talk about pedophilia?" Flemmi said, gesturing toward Bulger. "Right over there at that table."

It was obvious with each exchange that Flemmi was determined to insert Bulger's name wherever possible. He even tossed in an accusation that Bulger had a sixteen-year-old girlfriend that he took to Mexico, which Flemmi claimed was a violation of the Mann Act (also known as the White-Slave Traffic Act).

When Brennan began to address the Debbie Davis murder more specifically, he found additional discrepancies in Flemmi's prior testimonies. He either met Debbie at his parents' house, or he drove her there. He was either in front of her or behind her when Bulger strangled her. She either died upstairs or in the basement. Flemmi had told several different versions of the tragic event.

"Where did she die, Mr. Flemmi? Upstairs or downstairs?" Brennan asked.

"All I know is he strangled her. I'm not a doctor. She looked dead to me. She felt dead to me. She was dead. I didn't listen to her heartbeat. I'm not a doctor to testify that she was clinically dead. I'm telling you what I believe."

Flemmi also believed that he shouted "Let her pray!" at some point, but again, he couldn't be certain if he said it upstairs or downstairs, or if she was already dead at the time. "I blurted it out," Flemmi testified. "That was just a reaction on my part. As far as I'm concerned she was dead."

"You just shouted out, 'Let her pray!'?" Brennan asked incredulously.

"I might have said it upstairs or downstairs. That's exactly what happened. And nothing's going to change that. It's a guilt trip all these years that I'm on."

Next, Brennan attacked Flemmi on his motive, and Bulger's alleged motive. Flemmi swore Bulger killed her because she knew they were informants, but as Brennan pointed out, so did

Flemmi's parents. They were there when Flemmi and Bulger met with John Connolly at their house. Flemmi's mother cooked dinner for them several times.

"Nothing happened to your parents, did it?" Brennan asked.

"You mean, did I kill my parents? I don't even want to answer that question. It's such a ridiculous question." Flemmi also dismissed the notion that he killed Debbie out of jealousy. He said that he told Debbie she could leave any time she wanted, and if he were really the jealous type, he wouldn't have sent her on vacations where she could meet other people. He said she told him about Gustavo in Mexico, and that "of course, you get a little jealous, but not enough to kill her."

"Did you cry in front of the family?" Brennan asked, referring to the Davis family.

"No, I didn't cry."

"Did you tell them you would hire a private investigator?"

"That was all part of the cover up."

"Did you tell Olga Davis that Debbie had flown out of Logan Airport?"

"When you commit a murder, you don't tell people about it. I don't know if you're aware of that. You should be. You're an attorney."

Nearing the end of his cross-examination, Brennan reminded the jury, as he and Carney had done with Weeks, Martorano, and John Morris, that these prosecution witnesses had all received either immunity or plea bargains. It was Brennan's final effort to state categorically that these witnesses were motivated to provide substantial information whether it was true or not. In Flemmi's case, he avoided the death penalty, which led to this memorable exchange.

"You didn't want to die, did you Mr. Flemmi?"

"It wouldn't have mattered. I've survived a lot of other things."

"You would have survived the death penalty, would you?"

"I don't think I would have."

Some spectators in Courtroom 11, and others watching on closed circuit television in other courtrooms throughout the building, laughed out loud. Flemmi's perception of right and wrong was bizarre enough to be both horrific and, at times, humorous. His testimony, for example, suggested he thought it was crazy to think he could kill his parents, but not so outrageous to kill his stepdaughter and girlfriend, or anyone else for that matter.

"If somebody was a threat to you, you'd eliminate them?" Brennan asked.

"That goes without saying," Flemmi again responded as if the question were more absurd than the answer. Nearly every response Flemmi gave revealed something about his nature, and by the time he was through, the jury knew he was many shades of despicable, but worst of all for the prosecution, he was untrustworthy. Flemmi was the prosecution's star witness. Their intention was to link him to Bulger. *Look at Flemmi*, Wyshack seemed to say, *Everything he is, Bulger is, too. They were two sides of the same coin.* And the jury may have believed that, but they couldn't believe much of anything Flemmi said.

The discrepancies in his testimony about the deaths of Debbie Davis and Deborah Hussey were just the beginning. He also claimed he was either in front of Bulger on the basement stairs, or he was in the kitchen when Bulger shot Bucky Barrett in the head. He said Bulger approved the Wheeler murder from a payphone in South Boston, but he couldn't remember where the phone was, or specifically what Bulger said. Brennan successfully pointed out Flemmi had lied under oath many times before, so how could the jury trust he was telling the truth about anything now?

The entire time Flemmi was on the stand, the mystery of Steven Rakes's death went unsolved. Finally, about ten days after Rakes's body was discovered, police announced they had a suspect. They arrested and charged William Camuti with assault with intent to murder. They claimed Camuti owed Rakes a substantial amount of money, and that instead of paying him, Camuti killed him by lacing Rakes's iced coffee with two teaspoons of potassium cyanide. Police believe Camuti drove Rakes around for a few hours waiting for him to die, and then dumped the body.

"It's sad," Steve Davis said. "The guy was full of life."

CHAPTER THIRTEEN

The Right to Remain Silent

As July turned to August and the trial was about to enter its eighth week, there were only a few more witnesses left on the defense list. The great mystery remaining was whether Bulger would testify, and the defense was offering no clues. Steve Davis and the other victims' family members talked about it openly, and the jury had to be wondering as well.

There came a moment when Bulger's attorneys, who usually flanked him on either side at the defendant's table, were at a sidebar with the judge and the prosecution, and Bulger sat alone. His elbows rested on the arms of his chair. He stared at his fingers loosely clasped in front of his chest, and the jury stared at him. In addition to wondering if Bulger would testify, jurors may have also been struck by this old man sitting before them, a lonely figure who in a very real way was not alone at the table. By now it was clear that Bulger was not the only one on trial. The defense consistently made sure the U.S. government, and in particular the FBI, sat as co-defendants in this case. That strategy was a constant thread throughout the trial.

The FBI was on trial when Flemmi testified that former Special Agent Paul Rico tipped him off about the Fitzgerald bombing indictment. It stood accused when retired Special Agent John Morris admitted to setting up Brian Halloran, and again when Morris leaked information about a wiretap on a bookie named John Boharian, telling John Connolly he didn't "want another Halloran." The FBI was on trial when Morris and Connolly helped get Bulger and Flemmi's names out of the Race Fix indictment. Even the prosecutors themselves, Wyshack and Brian Kelly, were on trial for the deals they cut with the likes of John Martorano, Kevin Weeks, and John Morris, who not only received immunity from prosecution, but still receives a full pension from the FBI.

So, when Bulger shouted out during Morris's testimony, "You're a fucking liar!" there were many in the courtroom who agreed, and some were appalled as much by the FBI as they were by Bulger. The more the defense exposed the systemic FBI corruption, the more the victims' family members silently cheered. They wanted the prosecution to win and put Whitey Bulger away forever, but they found themselves in the conflicted position of rooting for the defense to at least score some points in their battle against the government. For that reason, a surprising and strong bond formed between the families and the defense counsel during the course of the trial. In their efforts to expose the criminality and the culpability of the FBI, these unlikely allies were on the same team.

Steve Davis still saw the FBI as the enemy, and there was a thick coating of distrust as he confronted Matthew Cronin, the FBI agent who had met several times with Steve's mother after Debbie went missing. Steve walked up to Cronin one day outside the courtroom and demanded to know why Cronin had met his mother in seedy hotel rooms and back parking lots. Cronin said that was for security reasons, which was similar to the testimony he would give a few minutes later.

"We didn't want to put her in harm's way," Cronin said in the courtroom.

Hearing what he believed to be a lie quickened Steve's heart rate. He seethed as Cronin contradicted himself on the witness stand. Cronin said he didn't want to endanger Olga Davis, but he had asked her to call Flemmi and accuse him of harming her daughter. Cronin said he had wanted to tap Olga's phone while she tried to get Flemmi to incriminate himself. Wouldn't that have put Olga in harm's way?

Cronin said he never went to the Marconi Club where Debbie was last seen because it was a missing person's case, and he had no jurisdiction, but then he met with Olga six times, each time telling her he was looking for Debbie.

"You were trying to get information from Mrs. Davis on Mr. Bulger and Mr. Flemmi, true?" Brennan asked Cronin.

"Yes."

It was a short reply, but it stung Steve Davis like a short jab to the kidneys. The truth he had always known was just confirmed: they had never looked for his sister. They had only used his mother. The veiled threat that Cronin or his partner, James Crawford, had said to his mother so long ago came back to Steve: "Don't forget you have eight other children."

Steve knows in his heart who's responsible for the death of his sister—Flemmi and Bulger—but he also knows who's responsible for the pain he's carried with him for more than thirty years—the FBI and the state police who never offered him the comfort of closure and justice.

He was angry as he drove home from the courthouse that day and angrier still when traffic on the expressway slowed to a crawl. But he reached a boiling point when he saw Bulger's motorcade parting traffic like Moses and the Red Sea. The sirens blared and cars moved to the left and right.

"Like he's the fucking president," Steve barked, as he quickly crossed over three lanes and got in behind the motorcade. He sped up and followed closely behind for a few hundred yards before he was cut off by another car. Steve said he was merely trying to beat traffic, but the federal marshals, who recognized him behind the wheel, wondered if he was chasing Bulger with bad intentions. So, the marshals paid him a visit at his home later that day.

"You think I'm gonna try to get to Bulger like that?" Steve asked incredulously. "I sit right behind him every day in court."

Steve was there again the next day as the trial came to a close. John Martorano was recalled to the stand for one brief line of questioning from the defense regarding Debbie Davis.

"Did Steve Flemmi tell you what happened?" Carney asked.

"He said she's gone. He said she's not coming back."

"Did you ask Steve Flemmi what happened, and didn't he say, 'I strangled her. It was an accident'?"

"My best recollection, with the encryptions, that's what I took out of it. He said it was an accident. He strangled her."

As disreputable and repugnant as Martorano showed himself to be during the trial, these last words of testimony may have been enough to plant the seeds of reasonable doubt in the jury's mind. Even though Martorano said he and Flemmi talked in code on the phone, and that's "what he took from it," the jury now had a contradictory version of Debbie Davis's death, and no evidence or credible witnesses.

It's been a trial of lies, Steve Davis thought. *Everybody knows what this guy was like, but are we going to get justice?*

That remained to be seen, but what Davis didn't get was his chance to hear from Bulger himself. Immediately after Martorano stepped down from the witness stand, the trial recessed for about fifteen minutes. Carney and Brennan met alone with Bulger, and he announced to them his decision—he would not testify.

Back from recess, but with the jury still out of the room, Bulger stood before Judge Casper and confirmed it was his choice not to testify on his own behalf.

"Did you make this choice voluntarily?" Casper asked.

"I'm making the choice involuntarily," he said surprisingly. His voice quivered a bit, perhaps out of nervousness or suppressed anger. "I feel like I've been choked off from giving an adequate defense, and to explain about my agreement with Jeremiah O'Sullivan. For my protection of his life, in return, he promised to give me immunity."

"That was my ruling," Judge Casper said. "I understand, sir, if you don't agree with it."

"I do disagree," Bulger said with added emphasis. "That's the way it is. As far as I'm concerned, I didn't get a fair trial. This is a sham. Do with me what youse will." Bulger's head dropped slightly, his fingertips pressing lightly on the table. He looked and sounded like a defeated man ready to accept his fate, but there remained an air of defiance and deceit about him. Despite all the evidence laid out before him, Bulger still believed the alleged promise of one man had given him the liberty to sell drugs, extort money, and even to kill. It was a delusional amount of either stupidity or hubris, but he stood there believing it.

Patricia Donahue believed something else. "You're a coward!" she shouted from the gallery.

Bulger ignored the insult, looked back up at the judge, and
said, "That's my final word."

Outside the courtroom Patricia Donahue explained why
she wanted Bulger to testify. "You kill all these people," she
began. "Then you go to trial and try to blame it on the Justice
Department and say, 'I didn't get a fair trial.' Well, get up there
and tell us that. I wanted to hear about all the government corruption. I was very disappointed."

There was that thread again. Patricia knew if Bulger had testified the world would have tuned in and the government corruption that helped get her husband killed would be exposed
to the masses. Bulger deprived her of that, but Carney and
Brennan picked up the baton and ran with it in their closing
arguments.

On Monday, August 5, Whitey Bulger walked into the
courtroom wearing a grey shirt and blue jeans. He went unno-
ticed by the victims' family members who were already sitting
in the courtroom talking about how restful their weekends had
been knowing the trial was about to end.

"Did you get truth in this case?" Hank Brennan asked the
jury. "Did you hear justice? Is there fairness in this case?"

There would be no denials of Bulger's guilt in Brennan's
closing argument, only accusations tossed at the government's
complicity and continued discrediting of the prosecution's key
witnesses. Brennan reminded the jury that John Martorano
was a killer whom the government had put back on the street,
that John Morris was a "habitual liar" and a "criminal," and
that the government made Steve Flemmi's attempted murder
charge against Fitzgerald go away so he could return and be
an informant for the FBI. Brennan said the FBI had a pattern

of corruption that was "common" and "consistent." "This is the way they operated," Brennan said. "Our government is not them. Our government is us. Those families, the Donahues, the Davises, they're our government. You are our government, and you have a voice. This government is accountable. You tell them that."

It was an impassioned speech, and the jury appeared intensely focused throughout, but Brennan never addressed anything truly relevant to the case. It would have been appropriate for the jury to think, *So what if government corruption helped facilitate Bulger's criminal behavior? He's still guilty of committing the crimes.*

J. W. Carney took over the second half of the closing and he returned to attacking the credibility of the witnesses. He contended that if the jurors couldn't believe Martorano, Weeks, and Flemmi beyond a reasonable doubt, then "the government can not prove its case about the alleged murders." Then Carney proceeded to attack the integrity of the prosecution's Big Three one by one. He called John Martorano a psychopath who added Bulger's name "like a spice" to every crime. He reminded the jury that Martorano had said it broke his heart when he learned Bulger was an informant, but added, "I think if you did a cat scan you'd have a problem finding his heart." Carney called Weeks a thug, and mocked him by telling the jury Weeks's nickname was "Two Weeks" because it only took him two weeks to turn over on his friends and make a deal with the government. "He told you, 'I'm a criminal. I lie,'" Carney said, adding, "May I kiss you, Mr. Weeks, for your candor? And the government wants you to trust him that he is telling you the truth."

Carney saved Flemmi for last and suggested that Flemmi sounded as if he were "following a script someone wrote for him." Like Martorano and Weeks, Flemmi, he said, went out of his way to throw Bulger's name into the mix whenever possible. "What was the weather today?" Carney asked with a playful lilt in a fabricated exchange with Flemmi. "It was raining— and Jim Bulger was my partner. What about this particular act, this crime, and were you alone? Yes, but Jim Bulger was my partner."

The prosecution broke with standard practice and legal etiquette and objected to Carney's tone, calling it unprofessional, but it was overruled.

The prosecution also objected when Carney claimed, "The government is buying the testimony of these witnesses. It sounds pretty awful to put it that way, doesn't it? The witnesses are selling their testimony, and the currency is how much freedom is the person going to get."

Carney spent some of his time specifically discussing the murders of Deborah Hussey and Debbie Davis, which seemed to confirm Bulger's desire to be cleared of those killings. Carney assigned the stronger motive in each murder to Flemmi. He said Flemmi killed Hussey before she could tell more people about his sexual relationship with her, and that he killed Debbie Davis before she could leave him.

"Remember what her brother Steven said was the way Flemmi viewed Debbie. She was his prized trophy," Carney said. "And now Debbie was going to end the relationship against his wishes. And then she disappeared."

Steve Davis's breathing got heavier. He looked at Carney and then at the jury. He believed, as the jury probably did, that Flemmi was more likely the hands-on culprit in his sister's death, but he also believed, and he hoped the jury would, too, that Bulger was present at the murder and, therefore, equally responsible.

"You don't have to decide who strangled Debbie Davis," U.S. Attorney Fred Wyshack had already explained during his closing argument for the prosecution. "What you need to decide is whether Mr. Bulger has any criminal liability in this murder. He doesn't have to be the one who strangled her. If he aided and abetted, he's as guilty as if he is the one who strangled the life out of her."

Steve could only hope the jury understood that legal nuance and didn't get lost in the defense's red herring regarding government corruption.

"The federal government is the most powerful force on earth in terms of government," Carney said, returning to the anti-government theme. "But there is one instance where a small group of people can stand up to the federal government. You are those folks. Members of the jury, I ask you to find strength in the oath you took. You have the power to stand up to our government's abuse. You can have the strength and power to come back and say 'No, we don't find the evidence to have been proven beyond a reasonable doubt.' Then you will embody our constitutional protections."

Like Brennan before him, Carney's closing argument had genuine passion and a degree of theatrics. It also had elements of truth and potential effectiveness. Carney's appeal to the jury hinged on the question: If the star witnesses sometimes lie, can they ever be believed? Prosecutor Fred Wyshack was confident he had already successfully addressed that question, and any other reasonable doubts the jury might have, during his closing. He didn't shy away from the issue of government corruption.

"It's disturbing that it was happening while they were informants for the FBI, and it happened right under the FBI's nose," Wyshack acknowledged. "It's disturbing that Mr. Bulger and Mr. Flemmi bribed FBI officials and other law enforcement, and were able to escape prosecution for so many years. It's disturbing that we're here twenty years later because Mr. Bulger was tipped off by John Connolly and he fled Boston, and remained a fugitive for all these years. Whether or not Mr. Bulger and Mr. Flemmi were informants has very little to do with the charges in this case. It doesn't matter if he was an informant when he put a gun to the head of Arthur Barrett and pulled the trigger. Whether he's an FBI informant or not, he's guilty of murder."

"This trial is not about whether John Morris and John Connolly were corrupt FBI agents," he continued. "It's about whether or not the defendant is guilty of the charges in the indictment. He's the one who's on trial here. Not the government, not the FBI, not John Martorano, not Kevin Weeks— James Bulger. You need to keep your eye on the ball. Don't get distracted by defense arguments."

A large portion of Wyshack's closing was similar to a tutorial on U.S. criminal law in which he played the role of the professor. He explained there are three ways a person is criminally liable: 1) as the principal actor who commits the crime, 2) as an aider and abettor who helps the principal, or 3) as a co-conspirator who is liable for every crime committed that is reasonably foreseeable within a criminal enterprise. Wyshack told the jury that if they found Bulger was the leader of a criminal organization, he was guilty of every reasonably foreseeable crime committed by any member of that organization. The notion of "reasonably foreseeable" would become an issue for the jury during deliberations.

"The evidence at this trial has convincingly proven that James Bulger is one of the most vicious, violent, and calculating criminals to ever walk the streets of Boston," Wyshack asserted.

"Mr. Carney told you in his opening that Mr. Bulger gave money to John Connolly. He told you his client was involved in loansharking, drug dealing, extortion. We don't dispute that. We agree with that. The evidence has shown that. He told you Mr. Bulger made millions of dollars engaging in this activity. We agree."

Wyshack made sure to point out that "Stephen Flemmi is a depraved individual," and then he linked Flemmi to Bulger, saying they were "two peas in a pod. Everything you might say about Stephen Flemmi, you might just as well say about Jim Bulger," Wyshack said. "Jim Bulger wants to distance himself from Mr. Flemmi. He can't do it. The same is true for John Martorano. For everything you want to say about them, he's the same."

Wyshack repeated that Bulger couldn't distance himself from Flemmi and Martorano, but in a twist, Wyshack tried to distance *himself* from those two criminals. For example, in an effort to explain why the government didn't insist Martorano get life in prison, he said they didn't have the evidence to put him away, but Martorano had information they needed to put Flemmi and Bulger behind bars forever.

"The relationship between Steve Flemmi, Jim Bulger, and John Martorano was a cancer eating away at law enforcement in Boston," Wyshack told the jury. "Bodies had piled up. South Boston had been flooded with drugs. The last insult of it all was Mr. Bulger had been allowed to escape, because he had been tipped off by a corrupt FBI agent. The only thing worse than making a deal with John Martorano at that time was not making a deal. The government held their nose and made that deal."

Next, Wyshack went down the entire list of murders, reminding the jury of the key evidence in each one, adding, "These men didn't hunt animals. They hunted people."

When Wyshack got to the Paul McGonagle murder, he said, "Mr. Bulger may as well have thrown his license into the hole with Mr. McGonagle. The man was buried in 1974. It lay there for twenty-six years. The only people who knew where it was were the people involved. And how is that body recovered? That body is recovered because Mr. Bulger told Kevin Weeks where that body was." Just in case the jury thought Weeks knew where the body was because he had committed the murder, Wyshack told the jury to consider that Weeks was in high school in 1974.

If the jury was to find Bulger guilty of killing Paul McGonagle, they might also be expected to find Bulger guilty of killing Bucky Barrett and Deborah Hussey because those three bodies were found in the same unmarked grave across from Florian Hall. "That's no coincidence," Wyshack said. And to further connect the dots, if the jury believed Bulger killed Deborah Hussey, they might also believe he killed Debbie Davis.

"What do you know about Mr. Bulger?" Wyshack asked. "You do know that he strangled Deborah Hussey. Mr. Flemmi was there, as was Kevin Weeks. When deciding who strangled Debbie Davis, you can consider who strangled Deborah Hussey. Mr. Flemmi said he didn't have it in him. Now, you can accept or reject that as you will. But that's a piece of evidence you can use to decide if he's the one that strangled Debra Davis."

Furthermore, if Hussey didn't connect Bulger to Debbie Davis, Thomas King could. Debbie's body was buried sixty feet away from King's. Wyshack called that fact "independent forensic evidence." He could make the same claim regarding Bucky Barrett. Witnesses said Bulger shot him in the back of the head, and when Barrett's skull was recovered, it showed evidence of a gunshot wound to the back of the head. Nearly three hours into his closing, Wyshack was beyond the time allotted by the judge. So, he raced through the extortion, drug dealing, and weapons charges, and then concluded, "The evidence in this case is overwhelming. The government has proven beyond a reasonable doubt that the defendant was one of the leaders of one of the most ruthless criminal organizations ever in Boston. It wreaked havoc on this city for decades. The defendant is personally responsible for much of the criminal activity committed by this group, including murder, extortion, money laundering, firearms offenses and drug trafficking. In his capacity as the leader, he is legally responsible for it all. I submit to you that after you've reviewed all the evidence in this case and you've deliberated, there is only one verdict that you can truly return. That is for a verdict of guilty on each and every count of the indictment."

Brennan and Carney followed Wyshack with their closing arguments, and then Wyshack was given fifteen minutes for rebuttal. When it was all over, Steve Davis quietly applauded. He watched Bulger, who was the last one to rise, and then quickly left the courtroom. He thanked the attorneys on both sides, and almost immediately began to worry about the verdict.

"Mine," Davis said, referring to justice. "I want mine. My sister—let her rest in peace. If the jury comes back with a not guilty on Deb's murder, I'll have to deal with that. I'll have to live with that. But if I didn't follow this through right to the end, I'd have felt like I sold her out."

The closing arguments were on a Monday. The jury received its instructions and a seven-page verdict form on Tuesday morning and they began deliberating that afternoon. Steve gathered with several victims' family members outside the courthouse that day, everyone offering their own estimates about how long the jury would be out. It was a complicated case with thirty-two indictments that included nineteen murders going back forty years. They were all prepared for this to take a while.

"We're all going to be on edge until a verdict is in," Steve said with a smile to unanimous agreement.

The jury deliberated for five painstakingly long days.

CHAPTER FOURTEEN

No Finding, No Closure

There's a black cloud over our heads as soon as they came into my family. My father died. My sister. My brother, Ronnie, died. It just kept going. It's not going to leave until they're gone.

—Eileen Davis

On the third day of jury deliberations, Steve and Maryann Davis stood together in the atrium of the Moakley Courthouse. Through the large windows that spanned all the way from the first floor to the ninth, they could see the sun shining on the Boston waterfront. Its placid beauty stood in stark contrast to the ugliness of the crimes they had heard chronicled for nearly two months in the courtroom above them. Joined by members of the Donahue and Barrett families, Steve and Maryann held hands and walked into the warm, refreshing air outside. Meanwhile, inside the jury deliberation room there was chaos and controversy.

According to Juror Number 5, Scott Hotyckey, there were jurors who had pounded the table and slammed the door. One juror wanted off the case and stormed out of the room. The tension apparently stemmed from both disagreement and fear. Hotyckey said some jurors were afraid of retribution, openly expressing concern that Bulger, or perhaps Pat Nee, might do something to them if they found Bulger guilty.

"I think they were terrified," Hotyckey said.

When the deliberations began, there were some jurors who were ready to convict immediately, hoping the matter could be settled the first day, but the rest of the jurors wanted to proceed cautiously. They took their time and read over the charges in the indictment several times, and then read and tried to understand the corresponding law. Ultimately, there was debate on whether Bulger committed a specific crime, and if so, there was further debate on what specific law was broken.

The defense strategy of discrediting the key witnesses carried a lot of weight with a few jurors who said they couldn't believe anything John Martorano said. Martorano, of course, provided the eyewitness accounts in many of the 1970s murders, including those of Al and Joe Notarangeli, Michael Milano, Al Plummer, William O'Brien, and James O'Toole. Early on in the deliberations, jurors appeared ready to convict Bulger of those murders, but with some members of the jury wanting to dismiss Martorano's entire testimony, it became increasingly difficult for them to reach a consensus.

Also dismissed was the defense's attempt to put the government on trial. That apparently had no bearing on the deliberations at all.

"Let's be honest," Hotyckey said. "Isn't it slightly treasonous to say the government is responsible for what Bulger did? When somebody tries to blame the government for somebody else committing murder, or a group of people committing murder and say that well, if somebody only got ten years [Martorano], and Bulger had to face all this [life in prison]—that's not really a defense."

Jurors agreed to work through the murder charges one at a time and to give Bulger the benefit of the doubt on each one. With nineteen murders to consider, and each juror speaking up and referring to his or her notes, the process was guaranteed to take a while. They moved into a fourth day of deliberations, which was a Friday, and a lot of lawyers, media, and victims' family members expected a decision before the weekend. They reasoned the jurors had already sacrificed their entire summer, and they wouldn't want to come back to court again on Monday. But, 4:30 p.m. came and went and still there was no verdict. It would be a long, anxious weekend for everyone involved.

"I'm scared in a way," Steve Davis said. "You can't predict what twelve people are gonna say."

Not surprisingly, the most difficult deliberations centered on Debbie Davis. The jurors were deadlocked and discussions grew contentious. Some jurors believed Bulger was guilty of at least being present at the time of the murder and therefore criminally responsible. Others presumed Bulger wasn't the kind of man who would kill a woman, which was a strange position to take, because those same jurors believed he killed Deborah Hussey.

"After you listen to everything," Hotyckey explained. "It's very easy to come to conclusions that the Debbie Davis murder was a normal course of business. I believe that yes, would they kill a woman because they felt it would affect their money, or bring attention to them? It seems to me very plausible."

Monday morning came and went. Jurors were entering their thirty-third hour of deliberations when suddenly there was a palpable shift in the energy around the courthouse. The jurors had sent a message to the judge. They had a verdict. Steve Davis would call the next thirty minutes "jaw crunching." He was among the first to return to the courtroom and he grabbed a seat in the front row. When the jurors entered, he looked at each of them closely. He didn't like that some of them were looking back at him. What did that mean? Steve took it as a bad sign.

To the surprise of no one, Judge Casper immediately called a sidebar with counsel from both sides. There had certainly been a lot of such sidebars throughout the trial. Bulger again sat alone. He flipped through the pages of his legal pad, appeared to find a blank page in the middle, put on his glasses, and began writing. He had less than a minute before the sidebar ended and Judge Casper addressed the court.

"I remind everyone in the gallery there will be order in the courtroom during the reading of the verdict, and its aftermath," Casper said sternly, and then turned to the jury. "Have you reached a unanimous verdict?"

"Yes."

At that moment, Steve Davis's heart pounded, and his hands shook just a little. He inhaled slowly, and exhaled in a quick burst. He hoped he'd be able to control his emotions. He believed the jurors' thirty-three hours of deliberation meant they had done their due diligence, and he was prepared for either a guilty or a not guilty regarding his sister's murder. Steve had waited a long time for this, but he would have to wait a few minutes longer.

There was very little movement and even less noise in the courtroom as the clerk, Lisa Hourihan, went over the seven-page verdict form to confirm the jury had completed it. When she was satisfied, Hourihan began to read the verdict.

"As to count one, racketeering conspiracy," she said. "Guilty."

Bulger, standing between his lawyers, didn't move. There was no discernible reaction either from him or the courtroom. Hourihan continued with Count Two.

"Guilty," she said again.

Count Two was also a racketeering charge, and it included the murder charges. To find Bulger guilty of Count Two, the jury had to find him guilty of at least two of the nineteen murders. Hourihan read down the list. The first was Racketeering Act Number One—conspiracy to murder members of the Notarangeli group.

"Not proved," she said.

Racketeering Acts Two through Seven related to the murders of Milano, Plummer, O'Brien, O'Toole, Al Notarangeli, and James Souza. After each name Hourihan said, "Not proved."

Clearly, the jury had decided John Martorano's testimony had been worthless.

"Racketeering Act Number Eight—the murder of Paul McGonagle," Hourihan continued. "Proved."

Next was Eddie Connors: "Proved."

Thomas King: "Proved."

Francis Leonard: "Not proved." That was another instance where Martorano's testimony was the only piece of evidence.

Hourihan continued. "Racketeering Act Number Twelve—the murder of Richard Castucci: Proved.

Maryann Davis put her hand on Steve's back and stroked him gently. She knew the verdict on Debbie's murder was nearing. Debbie was Racketeering Act Number Fourteen.

". . . the murder of Roger Wheeler: Proved."

This was it. Steve looked again at several members of the jury. He could tell they were anticipating a reaction from him, but he couldn't guess if they were happy for him, or if it were something else.

"Racketeering Act Number Fourteen—the murder of Debra Davis: No finding."

No finding? Davis thought, *What the fuck is that?* Steve took the news like someone getting a flu shot. It hurt, but he was determined not to show it. He was proud of himself for staying calm and not letting that "son-of-a-bitch Bulger" see him react. Steve looked again at the jury trying in vain to figure out what had happened, who was on his side, and who was against him. He was left to sit there in a confused state for several more minutes. And his confusion only increased as the rest of the verdict was read aloud. The murders of Brian Halloran, Michael Donahue, John Callahan, Arthur Barrett, John McIntyre, and Deborah Hussey were all "proved." In the end, Bulger was found guilty of eleven murders and every other charge against him except for two specific extortions. He was found not guilty of seven murders, and the jury couldn't come to a unanimous decision on Debbie Davis.

"They thought Flemmi did it," said Hotyckey, about the holdout jurors. Hotyckey thought Bulger was guilty of Debbie's murder, but he said the holdouts wouldn't budge. "If you're a juror and you hear somebody else say they are not going to change their mind no matter what anyone else said, what are you going to do? No finding."

Steve Davis was left with an empty feeling that was hard to describe, and even harder to process. He was prepared to celebrate, or be angry, or sad, but it never crossed his mind the jury would leave him with nothing. "I'm right back where I was since 1981," Steve said. "Not knowing what happened. I mean, what is that to leave me with no finding?"

Steve handled the verdict gracefully and analytically, like an athlete doing a post-game interview after a difficult loss. He offered congratulations to the Donahue family and others, and accepted hugs and condolences from several friends. He even laughed with Cheryl Connors, who had yelled "Rat-a-tat Whitey!" at Bulger as the courtroom adjourned. It was a reference to Bulger making the sound of a machine gun when he talked about her father's death while his nephew visited him in prison. That tape was played during the trial, but the jury still found Bulger not guilty of the murder of her father. She and Steve were able to commiserate with smiles on their faces.

Steve was still smiling when he spotted Hank Brennan outside the courtroom. He bounded up to him and stuck out his hand. "Hey, if I ever need a lawyer, I want you," Steve said to one of the men who defended Whitey Bulger. "Can I get a discount?"

"The first one is on the house," Brennan said, and the two men walked arm in arm down the hall.

Once outside, Steve was met by the largest media contingency he'd ever faced. There were dozens of cameras, microphones, and strangers. But he also saw friends in that crowd. He had a special affection for the local media, in particular, as so many of them had been with him for years. They kept his sister's name alive, and always treated him with respect. This was a tough moment for him, but out of respect for them, he stopped and opened his heart. "I didn't expect no finding because I have to tell you all, I don't feel like he [Bulger] hands-on himself killed my sister, but I do know he was guilty of conspiring or taking part in the whole thing. The no finding is better than a not guilty. If I was a juror, I probably would have swung the same way. I can't stand him, but I really don't know. I think he was there, because I don't think he would have allowed it being twenty-five feet away from his brother's house."

It continues to be Steve's theory that Flemmi would have cleared it with Bulger before he committed a murder so close to Bulger's brother's house. So, whether Bulger was there or not, he would have been a co-conspirator, but the jury never connected those dots.

Steve vowed to keep fighting. He said he'd try to have Bulger tried for his sister's death in state court. He called Bulger a rat, and explained, "That's the lowest type of criminal there is." But all the tough talk was followed immediately by a small breakdown. Steve seemed to be going through the five stages of grief in whirlwind fashion.

"She knows," Steve said about his sister. "She knows." His tears began to flow, and it was several seconds before Steve could continue. His voice was child-like now. High-pitched and broken. "She knows I'm a fighter. And I'll be the last man standing." He wiped his eyes with his shirt and walked away from the reporters. Maryann was there to hold him. He had trouble regaining his composure, but when he did, there were just a few remaining sniffles, and then another abrupt change in emotion.

"Let's go to the Barking Crab!" he said loudly. It was time to eat.

But a late lunch would have to be even later because Steve consented to do a series of local and national interviews. It seemed to be therapeutic for him. He bounced from live shot to live shot with renewed energy, and the questions allowed him to probe deeper for answers. He was beginning to realize that the jury must have believed Flemmi acted alone in the death of Debbie Davis, and that his motive was jealousy. The jurors didn't hold Bulger accountable because Debbie Davis's death didn't have anything to do with Bulger's criminal enterprise. They dismissed the motive that she could reveal Bulger and Flemmi's status as informants. Therefore, Debbie's death was not a foreseeable act, as Wyshack had explained the law.

"Because of his partnership with Flemmi, I thought they might have gotten a guilty out of that," Steve reasoned. "Somebody's responsible. This is how I've lived the last thirty-two years, not knowing where, when, how. I gotta take that to the grave with me. Shame on him. Shame on anyone that's involved."

Further analysis only perplexed Steve more. The jury believed Bulger was guilty of five of the six murders that resulted in bodies being buried in and around Quincy. Debbie was the only exception. Steve wondered how the jury could find Bulger guilty of Thomas King, but not his sister who was buried only sixty feet away. Steve also assumed the jury would reach the same conclusion regarding the murders of his sister and Deborah Hussey. Either both or neither would result in guilty verdicts, Steve thought.

"There seemed to be a little more evidence in the Hussey case," Hotyckey explained. That evidence would be Weeks's corroborating testimony and the fact that Hussey was buried with two other murder victims. "I'm sorry for Mr. Davis that he didn't have that final decision," Hotyckey continued, "but it's a good thing Bulger's off the street and he's not going to be extorting people anymore."

Steve did find some comfort in knowing that both Bulger and Flemmi were going to spend the rest of their lives in jail. There was also some joy in knowing that Bulger failed to clear his name as a lady killer, an informant, and a drug dealer. It was a resounding defeat, but Bulger, or perhaps just his attorney, tried to spin it positively.

"Mr. Bulger was pleased with the way the trial went and with the outcome," Carney said with sincerity. "He was surprised that the jury would come back eight times with a finding of not proven or no finding . . . and it was important to him that the government corruption be exposed, and important to him to see the deals the government was able to make with certain people."

Confirming that the trial was more about the show, and pulling the curtain back on government corruption, Carney added, "Mr. Bulger knew as soon as he was arrested he was going to die behind the wall of a prison or on a gurney and injected with chemicals that would kill him. This trial has never been about Jim Bulger being set free."

Yet, Carney said Bulger intends to appeal. He added that Bulger has regrets about some of the murders, which would imply Bulger doesn't regret others. Carney further suggested Bulger may try to let his feelings be known to some of the victims' family members "sometime in the future."

Hank Brennan said there was a limit to how much the corruption in the criminal justice system could be exposed during this trial, but believes that story will be told in greater detail some day, perhaps by Bulger himself. What was he writing on that legal pad day after day? "I don't think you've heard the last word from James Bulger," Brennan said.

Nor has anyone heard the last word from Steve Davis. Bulger's sentencing is scheduled for November 13, 2013, and despite the no finding verdict in his sister's death, Steve will fight for the right to be there and deliver his impact statement.

"It's not over for me," Steve said. "It's not over until I'm in the ground. I have fight in me beyond a reasonable doubt."

ACKNOWLEDGMENTS

Because I don't do it often enough, I'd like to start by acknowledging the love and support I get from my wife, Eileen Curran. During the year it took to write this book, she did whatever was needed to help. Sometimes that meant offering words of encouragement, or simply giving me the time, space, and opportunity to write. More often, and particularly coming down the homestretch, it meant reading, editing, researching, and interviewing. It helps to have a great writer and journalist on my team.

Special thanks go out to Steve Davis. His passion, openness, and integrity are behind every word in this book. His wife, Maryann, was also very gracious and accommodating with her time. She not only helped me understand Steve a lot better, she also makes great eggplant parmesan!

Without my literary agent, Matt Valentinas, I would never have met Steve, and certainly this book would never have been written. Matt brought us all together, found a wonderful publisher, and worked behind the scenes on various important aspects of the book. He's deeply involved in publicity and social media platforms, and lots of other things I don't enjoy doing.

What I'd like a book editor to be is someone who is patient, but pushy, and brutally honest, but in the nicest way. The editor needs to be close to the work, but distant enough to ensure that it maintains its focus and its tone throughout. The best editors can figure out how to simultaneously follow the author's vision and lead the author to it. Holly Rubino is all of those things, and my experience working with her was wonderful and stress-free. She's also really good at grammar and punctuation.

I'd also like to thank Liz McDonough who spiced things up with her tremendous insight into the minds of gangsters and their girlfriends. It seems like nothing happens in South Boston without her knowing about it.

I never met Steve Davis's attorney, Paul Griffin, but his help and generosity were essential. He provided a few thousand pages of trial transcripts, depositions, and other legal documents that gave me the background knowledge I needed to go out and find many more documents and transcripts.

The information in this book comes from interviews and conversations, court documents, some institutional knowledge, and wherever noted, published newspaper and Internet reports.

And finally, a quick shout out to my kids for their constant inspiration. One of the reasons I take on big challenges is to show them that they should, too. Now, if anybody needs me, I'll be golfing!